CH01022567

If sustainable, net positive business is t
ety), why is it difficult? Why doesn't it l
the way? To answer that core question
see in how businesses and investments are managed. A more optimal path
is possible, but requires a new understanding of the dynamics of capital in
business, they say, and show how to invest and build for both net positive
and profitability in ways that seem impossible today.

Andrew Winston; sustainability thought leader and best-selling author (with Paul Polman) of *Net Positive*

Most thoughtful observers understand the capital formation process of our
economy is broken. Few understand how the flawed statistics lying at the
foundation of "high finance" has led us astray. Perhaps only Boyd and Reardon can illuminate how ergodic thinking shines a light on the path to a prosperous future by aligning our finance with the complexity of how all living
systems actually work: in dynamic balance, collaboratively.

John Fullerton; Founder Capital Institute, author *Regenerative Capitalism*

Graham and Jack offer a breakthrough ergodic strategy of investing based
on a key element of anti-fragility: combining the advantages of collaboration (resource pooling between multiple entities across all capitals) and
competition (resource accumulation within entities) to support ecosystems.
The take-aways are significant and possibly solve the scaling issue that perplexes the regenerative community. The method take cues from nature and
is proven with mathematics.

Lyn McDonell; President, The Accountability Group, Inc.

Business must become a true collaborative citizen delivering on society's
needs today. To do so business needs to recognise the inherent nonlinearity
and path-dependence of all living systems, including business itself. Graham and Jack's work on non-ergodicity in business is an important contributing voice. Their *ergodic investment strategy* allows unpredictability to
become an integral part of business strategy.

Ebru Kaya, Tanuja Prasad; founders of Regenerative Investing Theory and Community of Practice

There is tendency among decision-makers to focus on predictable developments by either making unpredictable future trajectories predictable or assuming unpredictability away. Graham Boyd and John Reardon correctly argue that unpredictability is the essence of life, and cannot be removed. Luckily, they show how unpredictability can be front and center of strategy. We need to use our collective imagination by embracing science fiction strategies for making impactful decisions in life and business. A must read!

Meelis Kitsing; Rector and Professor of Political Economy, Estonian Business School

Working within Impact Investing in Brazil, the pandemic gave me a powerful experience of how complex the world is, and how attached we are to trying to predict all possible scenarios—and then failing to do so. I often hear "The only thing we are sure about is that reality is going to be different from the Excel sheet." Collaborating and building stronger ecosystems that generate positive impact is not only going to make us more resilient to what comes next, but may be our only chance of survival.

Vanessa Reis; HR Manager in Impact Investing

Oops…they did it again! Graham and Jack are giving the reader another experience after their first best selling hit *Rebuild*—now we are in for a "Lucky" treat. Graham and Jack eloquently walk the reader through the concepts of a business being ergodic (few are) if the expected outcome of the capital growth processes over time is the same as the average of the totality of all possible states of the business at that time. Stop suffering inefficient and hidden capital losses. Highly recommended read.

Antonio Potenza; FRSA, MBA Oxford, CISL Cambridge, Founder of Proodos Capital and Fund4Impact, Serial Entrepreneur

This book is amazing, because it gives a new perspective on business plans: bringing luck, unpredictables, and black Swans under one strategy, showing how we can win with randomness by pooling, planning, and diversifying at all levels! All investors and entrepreneurs need to apprehend, digest, and understand. This book is a seed that will blossom with examples to further convince all.

Marc Castagnet; Impact Entrepreneur

The Ergodic Investor and Entrepreneur is a thought-provoking and insightful read that provides valuable advice and guidance for anyone looking to succeed in the future world of investing and entrepreneurship. Graham and Jack draw on their extensive experience to introduce the concept of ergodicity, which emphasizes the importance of understanding the long-term impact of probabilities and risks associated with investments and entrepreneurial ventures. A refreshing angle in our increasingly volatile world.

Bárbara Leão de Carvalho, PhD

Once in a while, a new concept emerges which illuminates a previously hidden area within corporate risk analysis. The Ergodic concept and methodology outlined in this book is one these lights which shines and delivers renewed insights to those whose minds are open such ideas. The Ergodic process also has psychological parallels for leadership in exploring, challenging and regenerating otherwise firmly held beliefs to help form renewed maps of the investment world, a task we all would agree to be well worth pursuing.

Robert Dellner PHD; author, *Integral Impact Investments*

We're increasingly connected, yet more isolated, both as people and as businesses. This book offers a different perspective that inspires us to connect differently to gain individual advantage from collective advantage in a world of increasing chaos. The concepts express in business and for individuals the very essence of how natural ecosystems thrive. A book that will bring new essential tools to investors, entrepreneurs, and decision makers to better navigate in a context of exponential opportunities.

Patrick Martel; Vice-President, Innovation Development, Technosub; innovation entrepreneur

We often tend to polarize our societal choices as either / or: the market or the state, competition or cooperation between businesses. What is lacking is the third level of integration: the practice and institution of the commons. This book reflects the return of this theme in business thinking, and is a highly necessary preparation for a world in existential risk.

Michel Bauwens; author *Peer to Peer: The Commons Manifesto*

We need to fundamentally rethink our investment paradigms, if capital markets are to play a more important role in financing transformative solutions to the world's biggest challenges. This book provides fresh insights about how capital providers across all asset classes can better leverage unpredictability and make use of new business opportunities in systemic investing. **Anja-Nadine König; Founder and Director of Social Impact Markets, Transformative Finance Expert, Facilitator and Mentor.**

It's time to come together. It's never been so true, so urgent; and so rewarding, if we put what Graham and Jack are offering us into practice. **Ted Rau; Sociocracy For All. Author of *Many Voices One Song* and *Who Decides Who Decides***

Harness the unpredictable. This statement jumped out at me immediately when I first skimmed through the book. How could this not be one of the most important strengths for business in today's polycrisis world, yet all focus on risk management is to attempt the impossible—make it all predictable. And then the surprises hit! While the book debunks competitive economics, its misperceptions and mathematically illogical assumptions, it's first and foremost a plea for diversified and collaborative businesses. It's adding a resilience message on how to prepare the transition to a regenerative and distributive economy. This book fixes false assumptions, and I'll add one of my own: the idea that we can still avoid collapse. We are already in collapse, and no-one can know exactly what additional and potentially exponential unpredictabilities that will bring. Showing us how to harness these for resilience makes this book extra relevant today. **Ralph Thurm; R3.0 Managing Director**

We've entered times in which virtually everything is changing. Business sometimes leads adaptation to this change—but from a science perspective, business is often incredibly slow to question the basic framing. For everyone who wants to understand business, and the economy of the future, this book is a great paradigm-shift. **Phoebe Barnard; Affiliate Professor, Univ. Washington, Associate, Univ. Cape Town; CEO, Stable Planet Alliance; former Chief Science and Policy Officer**

We stand at a critical juncture in the evolution of our species, with the potential for either great human flourishing or a nightmare beyond our imagination. It is in this context that I am grateful to acknowledge the contributions of Graham Boyd and Jack Reardon. Through their work, they have shown us a new way to leverage the powerful tools of capital to make a positive impact on the world. They have given us a map, showing us how to shift our consciousness and use ergodic thinking to include all of life while we use the tools of capital to contribute towards the path of planetary peace and abundance for all. I am deeply grateful for their insights, vision, and dedication to helping us dream a new dream.

Lawrence Ford; *Shaman of Wall St*, CEO at Conscious Capital and Scious, and Chair of Future Capital

"This is how we can build a viable bridge from today to a prosperous tomorrow" is Graham and Jack's message to us all. This resonated so strongly with me that I joined in co-founding Evolutesix, to build this architecture of a potential future. We've passed the 11th hour, it's up to all of us to transform each of today's business and investment paradigms driving needless waste of all our capitals. And the biggest transformation is to harness unpredictables by going from prizing pure competition to a blend of keen competition and keen collaboration.

Marie Schuster; co-founder, Evolutesix

THE ERGODIC INVESTOR AND ENTREPRENEUR

A GUIDE TO ERGODIC FINANCE

Graham Boyd and Jack Reardon

May 2023

Others have seen what is and asked why. I have seen what could be and asked why not.

—Pablo Picasso

Join our monthly webinars and mailing list at `bit.ly/Ergodic_IE`
Go to `evolutesix.com` for more to help you put this book into practice.

Published by Evolutesix Books, London, UK.

Paperback ISBN: 978-1-913629-19-9

Copyright © Graham Boyd and Jack Reardon, May 2023

The rights of Graham Boyd and Jack Reardon to be identified as the authors of this work has been asserted by them in accordance with the Copyright, Designs and Patents Act 1988.

RELEASE 1.0.1

A CIP catalogue record will be available from the British Library.

Typeset using LaTeX.
Cover by Nikyta Guleria
Editing by Anna Kierstan

Contents

There's a new strategy on the block, with a funny name: ergodic. It's an important, but little-known driver of some of the world's most successful companies. It's time for us all to use it.

Luck, skill, or strategy—which of these is more important to reach the peak of success? Whether success is investing in the next unicorn, founding the next unicorn, or winning a Nobel prize? Why do companies like Unilever more often stay steady during unpredicted global headwinds, while most single-purpose companies experience wild swings? How has, is, and will your whole life be shaped in ways you're not seeing?

Unpredictables are certain; the essence of life, including business. We humans have thrived because we learn new strategies when life takes us by surprise. Business strategies today are no longer fit for our unpredictable world, because we focus on prediction and control. It's time for a new strategy, neither aiming for complete control nor completely surrendering to chaos.

CONTENTS

Everything you've been taught about how capital changes in an unpredictable world is wrong. A useful business plan must start with ordered multiplicative capital change processes. If not, you're using the wrong equations to build the business plans you're using to take investment decisions, start your business, or even plan your own future.

These are the ergodicity-blind strategies that businesses and investors default to in order to compensate for the detrimental effects of our non-ergodic world, which cause unproductive capital loss. These default strategies have a role to play in business, but exacerbate the losses when used to compensate for ergodicity-blind strategies.

In which we test out potential strategies, fully informed by the non-ergodic nature of business, able to harness the unpredictables that impact capital. Let's first explore doing this perfectly in a science fiction universe, free of the limitations of physics, to see the essence clearly.

Inspired by the perfect science fiction strategy, you see what a practical strategy harnessing the unpredictability and variance in non-ergodic capital growth looks like. One you can start deploying in your business or investments today.

Here are the right equations for your business plans, because they represent real-world capital change processes: multiplicative and order-dependent. You'll see why business today preserves capital like a colander preserves water, and what you can do to plug the holes.

CONTENTS

8. BUILDING ERGODICALLY —— 74

Excellent execution of an ergodic strategy requires ergodically tuned structures, interactions, and governance. Want to start building them? Fortunately all you need to get started already exists; just use and optimise what we already use in novel ways.

9. WHY BIGGER *IS* BETTER —— 92

Why life on earth is antifragile at scale. Why business antifragility increases as the diversity of business types and scales, connected together into a profit-pooling ecosystem, increases. Even better is connecting these ecosystems into ecosystems of ecosystems. Take this all the way and we will have an antifragile, net positive, regenerative, profitable global economy.

10. YOUR LIFE —— 103

Ergodic strategies need ergodicity-minded and capable people. Harness the power of unpredictables in your life by applying an ergodic strategy to all of your capitals. Financial, of course—but also your self esteem, relationship, social, intellectual, knowledge, and all the other capitals that are valuable to your life.

11. VISION: AN ECONOMY MEETING ALL NEEDS —— 116

Before fully committing the effort and investment in building new business forms, maybe you want to see more clearly where they'll take you. As stated in *The Little Prince*, this chapter is about painting an inspiring picture of the world we can have after executing an ergodic strategy with excellence.

CONTENTS

12. CONCLUSION —— 126

The less control we have over the unpredictables in our future, the more we benefit from using ergodic strategies today. Attribute to no other cause that which is adequately explained by unpredictables in non-ergodic dynamics.

List of Figures

Preface

Life rarely unfolds exactly as we want it to. And if we stop and think about it, that makes perfect sense. The scope of life is universal, and the fact that we are not actually in control of life's events should be self-evident.

—Michael Singer[1]

There a little-known secret underpinning the success of companies as diverse as Apple, Unilever, Mitsubishi, and Mondragon.

We can all use this secret to deliver more with less capital.

Including making net positive natural.

If you're an investor—whether you're a large pension fund manager, in private equity or venture capital, a small angel, impact investor, or philanthropist—and whatever your mandate, this book shows how you can increase your return on investment, whatever your measure for return is.

If you're an entrepreneur of any flavour—purely profit driven, social, regenerative, etc.—this book shows how you can significantly reduce your risk of unnecessary business collapse and increase your success, whatever your measure for success.

If you are driven to solve humanity's biggest challenges through net positive, regenerative, sustainable, and circular business, but have yet to find a way that is also financially viable, this book shines a light on a new class of strategies that can deliver a healthy financial profit and even better deliver net positive, regenerative, sustainable, and circular outcomes.

This book is about a powerful strategy, which we're naming an Ergodic

Investment Strategy to stay in the game[2] for long enough to benefit from alpha. As Nassim Taleb said[3] in his criticism of Meng's decision in CalP-ERS: *What Universa is doing is allowing people to stay in the game long enough to gather alpha. It's not a luxury. It is a necessity.*

If you're saying to yourself *'the investment paradigm isn't perfect, but it only needs a few tweaks, there's nothing substantially wrong'*, ask yourself how high do you estimate the average ROI is for those buying shares in the 20 biggest IPOs of venture backed US startups founded in the 15 years prior to 2023? A recent Crunchbase article[4] states: a 42% loss! All were, when the analysis was done (May 2023) trading below their closing price on the first day of trading, and 17 were below their offer price. More on page 22.

As a simple introduction, imagine you're presented with an investment opportunity. The founder shows you a business plan, with some weeks growing[1] by 32.68%, and other weeks losing 30.00%. On average half the weeks deliver growth, and half the weeks deliver loss. You're asked to invest for 10 years. What exit does the business plan tell you to expect? The solid line in Figure 1, giving you an average 1.34% each week, i.e., doubling each year; or the dashed line, giving you no liquidity within five years?

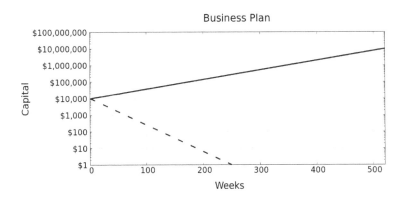

Figure 1: Should you expect to lose it all, or double in size each year? Note this is a log plot, so the lines are the well-known hockey sticks.

If you said *the solid line, the business doubles in size each year* you would be wrong.

---

[1]These are the parameters I've chosen throughout the book to illustrate the point.

This book is about why you would be wrong. And what to do to recover the naïve 100% annual growth rate: use a little-known class of strategies that we call ergodic strategies, because they get your business, or your investments, as close to the ergodic maximum (solid line) as possible. We'll unpack just what an ergodic investment strategy (EIS) is in Chapters 3 and 7. On page 60 is the full definition of ergodicity. For now, the simple definition: capital grows ergodically if the dashed line is on top of the solid line.

Here's a simplistic[2] illustration of what each line is, and why they can differ. Imagine you're on a chess board, with a different percentage number on each square, changing your bank balance up or down by that percentage.

Take two fair eight sided dice, and land on the square indicated by each toss. Your bank balance grows or shrinks by that percentage. If 10,000 people play the game, the total change to the bank accounts is $10,000\langle x \rangle$. This is the logic behind the solid line $\langle x \rangle$.

This changes if, instead of 10,000 people landing on each square at random, you're walking at random from square to square, according to the fall of your dice, for 10,000 steps in sequence. Each step takes you onto a different square. Now what matters is both the dice being fair and the dynamics allowed for moving. If you can only move forwards or backwards, you will only sample 8 of those squares, no matter how long you move for. The dynamics no longer gives access to all states. Your expected outcome after 10,000 steps, the time or path expected outcome, is clearly a different number to $10,000\langle x \rangle$. The dashed line is this time expected outcome. I'll explain this in more detail in Chapter 7.

There is a root cause that few fully understand behind the success of the companies listed in the opening lines, and of lossmaking investment and business strategies in most.

The big idea in an ergodic investment strategy may seem counterintuitive to you: a blend of hard competition and hard collaboration. Hard collaboration means that every company in a highly diverse ecosystem commits to putting a small fixed percentage of their profit (if they make one that year) into a central pool, which is then immediately shared out again to all companies in the ecosystem.

Nature uses an ergodic strategy, which is why life thrives regardless of

---

[2] This example over-simplifies most real life capital growth processes to only introduce path-dependency clearly. Chapter 7 gives the precise definition.

the detrimental unpredictables. The quote from Michael Singer[1] at the start of this chapter, and his success in business and life, is because he mimicked nature's successful ergodic strategy.

If you've worked in a large and long-successful multi-product corporation, the further you read in the book, the more you might recognise that a partial ergodic strategy (but one you were not consciously using) is partly behind your company's success.

In his 1996 book *The Death of Competition*[5] Moore gives compelling evidence for the advantage of a blend of cooperation and competition, but without the underlying mathematical and numerical clarity of ergodicity economics to define and execute the optimal blend for a given business.

> A note on language: read "I" in this book to mean Jack or Graham speaking for themselves, as well as Jack and Graham speaking with one voice. Occasionally, if it is one of us, say Jack, I'll write I (Jack). Equally "you" refers to you as one person reading this, and all of you reading this book. "We" primarily refers to everybody—including me (Jack and Graham). I'm also using a blend of British (e.g., different to, and take a decision) and American English in the book, as befits our personal paths through life.

I find the big idea discussed in this book exciting, because it enables each of the many different approaches to solving problems through the power of business to deliver more with less. Because it gives us a way of collaborating *for our own benefit* with groups we currently see as competitors.

The battle between financial returns and impact returns, between investors and founders, between staff and executives, between the environment and the economy, and many of the other battles, are unnecessary artefacts of flaws in our assumptions about how capital changes over time.

This book shows how we can do better by fixing the flaws[6] in our assumptions about what business, investing, and capital is. It provides scaffolding for investors, founders, and all other stakeholders across our society and economy to collaborate; even if they don't agree with nor like nor trust[7] the people they are collaborating with.

It's time to transform the needless waste across all of the six capitals[6] (financial, natural, intellectual, human, social, and manufactured) into the results we need.

I get some hope for the future because I have experienced just how much more we can achieve by working with, not against, the non-ergodic nature of business. Especially today, when it has become perfectly clear that we passed the 11th hour at least a decade ago. It is now the hour. I need—and likely you do as well—a grounded reason to hope that business today can deploy its power to multisolve our biggest challenges.

This book gives such a much-needed grounded message of hope[8]: we do not need to use all the resources we are using; and yes, there is a better way of achieving healthy financial returns on investment and net positive outcomes without compromise.

The big idea in this book is the key that unlocks the full potential of many vital approaches currently being implemented by innovative investors and entrepreneurs: *Net Positive*[9] promoted by Paul Polman and Andrew Winston; *Stakeholder Capitalism*[10] promoted by Schwab and Vanham; the regenerative economy of John Fullerton[11], Daniel Wahl[12], and Hunter Lovins[13]; the *Triple Bottom Line*[14] of John Elkington; circular[15] or blue[16] economy; Conscious Capitalism[17]; B-Corps[18] and public benefit corporations; for-purpose and steward-owned companies, as promoted by the Purpose Foundation's[19]; Peer to Peer commons-based business[20]; venture philanthropy and impact investing; multi-capital accounting[21]; and the intent behind many of the emerging DAOs and web3.0 like Regens Unite[22]. The list could go on, but for brevity I'll stop here, even though many more are doing vital work.

You'll also see that the big idea in this book shares common ground with the precepts and practices of many of the world's old faiths and indigenous cultures. These were shaped over millennia by cultural evolution: those groups that used ergodic strategies thrived. You'll recognise that the practices of putting a minimum percentage of your earnings, or your wealth, into a central pot for the community, is an ergodic strategy in action.

An unfair advantage our species has over all other kinds of life on the planet is our capacity to see patterns of cause and effect. Some other species do this, but we do it orders of magnitude better than any other species. Whenever I see a pattern, I see cause and effect. Quite often there is none, it's only in my imagination. I need to remind myself everything I know about randomness, including that, given enough time and no constraints on randomness, an infinite cage of monkeys hitting the keys at random will eventually produce the complete works of Shakespeare. Or this book.

This is at the heart of the big idea of this book: we're biased to discount the role of randomness, the role of unpredictables in our lives and our businesses, to see cause and effect even where there is none. We feel safer, and in control, believing that everything is inherently predictable, and that if we try harder we can predict everything. Because of that, we have unquestioningly accepted a false assumption in economics, leading to business plans that are systemically biased[6] to overestimate the upside and underestimate the downside outcomes of unpredictables.

We are too often using inappropriate simplified statistics to calculate expected outcomes, and so to predict probable future business performance; simplified statistics that are only valid if a certain assumption is true, i.e., the assumption of ergodicity. But it's false in the dynamics of almost all relevant capital growth processes in economics and business.

This false assumption about the dynamics of capital growth in business, and across our economy, hides from us the fact that we can, and will, get healthier long term financial returns because we make the economy as a whole net positive.

You might (unless you are already somewhat familiar with the topics introduced here) think *'but that must be wrong'*. Maybe it is; maybe it isn't! Even if you don't buy the core idea, please consider renting it (at zero interest!) until you reach the end of this book.

Abraham Maslow said *He that is good with a hammer tends to think everything is a nail.* Your success is quite likely because you're good at applying what you've come to believe works in business and investing. Now it's time to level up, change the game, from being an expert in hammers and nails to being an expert in nuts and bolts. And so I invite you: pause every time you think to yourself *'what I've just read must be wrong'*, write down what your truth is, and then ask yourself the following questions.

- How did I learn this truth of mine?

- When did I first learn this? Follow this question back to the earliest point in your life where you started learning this truth of yours.

- Who did I learn this truth from?
- Who else in my peer group also believes this truth?
- What could happen if I transformed this truth of mine to include what I've just read? Look here at both beneficial and detrimental outcomes. Especially anything linked to your identity, belonging, recognition by peers, and anything else that is valuable to you. (See *Rebuild* Part 3.)

I'm inviting you to pause judgement and ask these questions because I know that each of us believes what we believe because it has worked well for us, or our role models, in the past. And so we expect it to work well for us in the future. Or, perhaps, because it's the best you know of, even though you suspect it's not working well enough.

You'll read more in the subsequent chapters about the three types of evidence demonstrating the validity of everything in this book.

1. The maths. If you're going to use an equation to predict future outcomes, you'd better use an equation that fits the processes leading to those outcomes. Saying $1 + 1 = 10$ is valid if, and only if, you are using binary, not because you forcefully declare it to be true.

2. Nature. Wherever you look in nature, this is how nature delivers antifragility across aeons.

3. Business. Large companies like P&G, General Electric, and Unilever; Asian conglomerates, like Yamaha and Mitsubishi; traditional SMEs in a small town, and many small cooperatives joined together, like CCA partners and Mondragon; and the longest lasting, perhaps most successful business endeavour ever, the Hanseatic League, followed the ergodic investment strategy of this book, albeit without knowledge of the underlying reason why.

There is no doubt that business has done a lot of good, and hence why many successful investors and entrepreneurs today believe that how we invest, and how we start and run businesses today, is right and based on solid evidence. However, part of this belief is neither anchored in reality nor in solid evidence.

There is much in business studies and economics that is actually a cargo cult[6]. As World War Two raged, the Melanesian Islanders saw Japanese planes, and later American planes, bringing in supplies. Not understanding what was actually happening (a world war, the nature of flight, etc.) they began following rituals patterned on what they saw the troops doing before a plane brought supplies.

So they flattened strips of ground, built a hut in the middle, and wore coconut shells fashioned to look like headphones; but clearly these rituals are not going to cause an aeroplane with supplies to materialise! Richard Feynman named these rituals *cargo cults*.

As of December 2022[3], 500 people in the village of Lamakara on the island of Tanna are still adherents of one of these cargo cults. Cargo Cult describes something dressed up in fake evidence to give it legitimacy, but that is not actually evidence based, and lacking a solid cause-effect underpinning. Instead, it is rituals that create faith and attribute cause to random patterns. This can create spurious self-blame: it's not working because my belief is not strong enough, or I'm not trying hard enough, despite a lack of solid evidence.

Recognising a cargo cult vs. a concept truly supported by the evidence is one essential capability you need to gain first mover advantage at the start of a new disruptive wave transforming an entire sector.

Also have a look at my other book, *Rebuild: the Economy, Leadership, and You*[6]. (From now on I'll just write *Rebuild*.) In it you can find more about how our hardware (senses), firmware (natural talents, basic personality), and software (capacity to use binary logic and dialectic thought forms, plus our meaning-making) constructs our experienced reality, which we then often mistake for what is actually there, which I label actuality. And you'll learn about a powerful way of transforming how you construct your experienced reality, helpful when life is telling you it's time to adapt, or risk not making it.

Rebuild also covers the myths that have become concretised in the institutions of business and economics today, where mistaking them for truths is a big cause of our current polycrises.

Throughout this book you'll see graphs like Figure 1 with capital on the vertical axis. If your focus is on natural capital, life capital, or human capitals like intellectual, relationship, and many others, the concepts and

[3]https://en.wikipedia.org/wiki/John_Frum

graphs are equally relevant however the capital is represented: as a barrel of oil, a wallet of notes, or tokens of a DAO (Decentralised Autonomous Organisation) on the blockchain.

Apply this book to yourself as an investor regardless of the capital you're investing: reputation, time, intellectual, your self esteem, not just financial capital. So this book applies to your whole life as much as it applies to your work and your financial investments.

Whether you are an angel investor, fund manager, venture philanthropist founder, working in a company, a member of a family, or just living your life, this book is relevant to you, because you are investing in one or more of the six capitals. So please look at everything in this book through the lens of whichever of the six capitals you are most interested in.

Chapter 1 covers how and why, whatever success means to you, whatever wealth in the six capitals is relevant to your success, beneficial and detrimental unpredictables; luck, in other words; is far more important to your outcomes than you are likely to believe.

So long as you have the minimum talent to do a good enough job, the differentiator, the key success factor, is luck. Even winning a Nobel prize is, at the end, about luck rather than having more talent than any other contender (chapter 1).

So we need intelligent (effective and practical) strategies to work with luck, to harness unpredictables for our benefit.

When Napoleon said that he preferred to appoint lucky generals he was not in any way giving up on agency; rather, he recognised the irreducible role of unpredictables meant that the most useful agency a general can have is the ability to maximise the beneficial outcomes when responding to and shaping unpredictable events.

The insights and intelligent strategies in this book will give you two valuable benefits.

1. Grounded hope that the capitalism we have today is not the only kind of capitalism on the menu. Fixing the false assumptions that have given us the excessive costs of today's capitalism gives us what we need in order to multisolve[23].

2. Clarity on how unpredictables have, and always will, shape our lives in ways beyond our control; and what each of us can do to make

unpredictables work for us in the future. The remaining chapters lay the foundations, and Chapter 10 deals specifically with applying this book to your own life.

You'll see in this book why the sequence of events that have happened in your past have shaped the life you have today; and why collaboration, even collaboration with people you don't agree with nor like nor trust, is more likely to give you success than pure go-it-alone competition.

Throughout the book I mostly use the word unpredictables, rather than luck, as a neutral word that speaks to all meaning-making in this theme. I will unpack just what I mean with these words in Chapters 1 and 2.

We have entered a new geological era, the Anthropocene, an era where, at a planetary scale, the transformations created by humanity over the past two centuries are now the dominant driving force. The transformation of the planet has only just begun, far more is coming, and the path from here to there will be a sequence of unpredictables.

We homo sapiens can change fast because we have an unfair advantage over most other species. They can only respond to change at the speed of genetic, or hardware evolution. But we can learn new skills, facts, and success strategies at the speed of change, because we can transform our software—beliefs, meaning-making, etc. Proto-humans thrived because of this during the last ice age, the Pleistocene, by transforming our usage of the technologies of hammers, blades, and fire.

As McRaney writes: *Changing our minds became our greatest strength as a species.*[24]; or the essence of Jared Diamond's book[25] on why civilisations collapse: *the failure to [change when the environment does] may be our greatest weakness.*

Perhaps John Kenneth Galbraith put it best: *faced with the choice between changing one's mind and proving that there is no need to do so, almost everyone gets busy on the proof.*

The evidence is now unambiguous: change has started across the board, and we can no longer stop it. Our job as investors and entrepreneurs is to do the best we can to respond net positively.

And the biggest step is to change our minds. In the face of evidence that it is time to change one's mind, those few that change first will win disproportionately.

CHAPTER 1

Luck, skill, or strategy?

Most of our assumptions have outlived their uselessness.
—Marshall McLuhan

Better skills, better strategy, or more good luck—which is more often the differentiator in your successes?

Insufficient skills, bad strategy, or bad luck—which is more often the differentiator in your failures?

The surprising answer is luck!

However you've reacted, stay with me for a moment and look at what you mean, i.e., what you point at, with the word luck.

Luck is a word resembling a black suitcase, the kind you see cloned infinitely many times on airport luggage carousels. Each of us has packed our word with a wide range of different items, so even though your word is spelled the same as mine, the meaning each of us makes of the word is unique. So we need to unpack it.

Take a few moments to ask yourself the following questions, and perhaps refer back to them every time you read another of these suitcase words, where your understanding is quite likely to have differences to the meaning I'm trying to transmit.

First, ask yourself *'what does luck mean to me; what are the different kinds of evaluations I make when someone ascribes a beneficial or detrimental outcome to luck?'* Flesh out your answers to this question as much or as little as you find helpful. Then, ask yourself the questions listed on page xi.

To minimise the different interpretations of all of these meaning-making nuances that make luck a polarising suitcase word, most of the time I will use the word *unpredictables*. You can read much more about exactly what I mean in Chapter 2.

Let's first look at a few illustrations of just how big an impact beneficial and detrimental unpredictables have in successful businesses.

Take three quite different companies during 2020 and 2021, as the Covid-19 epidemic came in.

Procter and Gamble, the world's largest FMCG[1] company, had a market cap[26] of $308.43B on 31 December 2019, peaking at $393.53B on 8 January 2022. The market cap graph for the year from August 2020 to August 2021 looks pretty much like the kind of steady performance P&G is known for. Right now, on 8 November 2022, it's at $323.46B.

Zoom, the online meeting provider that filed its IPO on 18 April 2019 at a market cap of $9.2B, had a market cap[27] of $18.81B on 31 December 2019, peaking at $158.99B on 16 October 2020, and stayed above $90B from August 2020 to August 2021, and is back down to $23.7B on 8 November 2022.

Get Your Guide, which provides local travel guides, fared quite differently to Zoom during the pandemic. Get Your Guide managed to avoid collapse by laying off 100 employees, reducing expenses wherever possible, managing to raise $133M in a short-term convertible note on 29 October 2020, and securing a $97M revolving credit facility on 16 February 2021. This, after a $484M Series E on 16 May 2019 at a $1B valuation[28]. With travel now picking up, Get Your Guide's financials are looking healthy again.

These three companies had good strategies, good products, and skilled, talented staff. The big difference lay in unpredictables, especially Covid-19.

Of course it had long been perfectly clear that a pandemic was coming at some time. We'd had warnings with SARS-CoV-1 in 2002 and MERS in 2012. So the known unpredictables were: when the next coronavirus mutation would come, how infectious and deadly it would be, how governments would react, and how the world would be affected. Not if.

P&G, Zoom, and Get Your Guide could not have included, in their

[1]Fast Moving Consumer Goods

2019 shareholder reports, strategies, or investment round, the 2020 timing and impact on their businesses, and nor could their investors.

The impact on their cash flow and valuation was no reflection of the quality of their staff, leaders, or strategy.

Of course, how they dealt with Covid-19 does, in part, reflect the quality of their staff, leaders, and strategy. In particular, it reflects on their capacity to have an emergent strategy[6], one that flexes and flows in real time with current events filled with unpredictables.

Unpredictables played a decisive role in the near demise of Get Your Guide and the near complete loss of their investors' money; and equally in the gains of the investors in Zoom. In other words, beneficial luck for some and detrimental luck for others coming out of the same unpredictable. Had Covid arrived in 2017, 2022, or even 2030, funds backing each of those companies may have performed completely differently.

Procter and Gamble continued its more or less steady progress, across its 65 brands, 22 of them with over $1B in revenue. However, good as its strategy team is, I doubt that the arrival specifically of Covid-19 midway in the 2019-2020 fiscal year was explicitly included in the business plan.

P&G's progress was steady because, first, Covid-19 caused some brands (e.g., fabric and home care brands) to perform significantly above prediction counterbalancing those (e.g., beauty care) performing below prediction.

Second, because of the quality of the leaders, staff skills, and excellent contingency planning, and most especially the pooling of intellectual, relationship, and all the other human capitals[2], P&G is always prepared and able to react very quickly with a new, emergent strategy. For example, repurposing production lines for mask manufacturing.

P&G had no need to rapidly hire new staff, nor retrench large swathes of existing staff, nor seek significant unplanned emergency lines of credit.

Throughout this book we will draw further lessons from how these three companies fared during Covid-19 to bring to life how common unpredictables are, how they create dynamics in the performance of investment funds and investee companies over time, and what to do about them.

The single most important lesson is that our economy is filled with

---

[2] I often use the plural, capitals, to point clearly at the multidimensionality of human capital.

known, unknown, and even unknowable unpredictables.

When one of these works to your advantage it's commonly called good luck, and when one works to your disadvantage, bad luck.

Malcolm Gladwell writes that talent is over-rated[29]. An example of this, found in research by a collaboration between economists and physicists (Pluchina, Biondi, and Rapisardi), was published in *Talent versus luck: the role of randomness in success and failure*[30], and covered recently by a *Wall Street Journal* article entitled *Winning a Nobel Prize Takes Luck as Much as Talent*[31]. This shows clearly: the winner is unmistakably luck, not talent.

Pluchina, Biondi, and Rapisardi used an agent-based model commonly used by economists to understand what's important and what's not important. It starts with individual agents having a range of scores for their level of talent and skill, from unskilled and untalented to highly talented and highly skilled. Each agents then follows their own path through life, having, every so often, a random, unpredictable beneficial or detrimental experience. Over the course of each individual's life path, it became unmistakably clear: for those at or above the minimally sufficient level of talent and skill to act on the beneficial unpredictables they experienced, the final outcome was far more affected by the difference in the unpredictables than in their talents or skills. For example, a Nobel might have been won because one of the selection committee read a certain newspaper article that morning, instead of a different article.

This is just as true for investors[32], whether you manage a large fund manager or are a small angel investor. Better skills and strategy are important, but unpredictables make the difference. In fact, one of the few in finance who grasps the theme of ergodicity, Joe Wiggins, states in his book *The Intelligent Fund Investor* that randomness and chance led to his successful career in fund research.

Across multiple cultures and faiths there has long been an understanding of the inherent unknowability, unpredictability, and mystery inherent to everything in the universe. Daoism states that the Dao that can be named is not the Dao. I paraphrase that in business as:

> *the strategy that can be named is not the strategy.*

So the intelligent investor makes unpredictables work for them, not by trying to eliminate mystery and unknowability, but instead by using their skills and talents to create conditions that maximise the probability and size of beneficial outcomes, while minimising the impact of detrimental outcomes emerging from unpredictables. The intelligent entrepreneur creates the conditions for benefitting from good luck and minimising the losses from bad luck, looking at the entire duration of their investment.

Of course, this doesn't mean that everything is luck. You need to have a strategy that is good enough, you need to have skills that are good enough, and you need to have sufficient natural talent. If any is insufficient, your fund, and the startups you invest in or create, are likely to fail.

Once you have sufficient talent, skills, and strategy, improving business performance by getting even more skilled, hiring even better talent, or revising your strategy again is a game of diminishing returns, compared to creating structured luck. In other words, maximising beneficial outcomes from unpredictables. Your best bet is to work on the structures and interactions that maximise the benefits when good luck comes your way, and increase the odds of good luck coming your way. And conversely, minimise the detrimental consequences when, and decrease the odds of, bad luck coming your way.

There is solid science behind this, which we will discuss in the coming chapters, along with concrete actions you can take to make the science of luck work for you.

Paul Ormerod in his book *Why Most Things Fail: Evolution, Extinction and Economics*[33] describes his research, and that of others, on company failures spanning a century, from small enterprises to large multinationals, and found that the only explanation that fitted the data was randomness. A sequence of unpredictable events, or maybe just one big one, that removed the company from existence.

We seldom have any way of knowing for certain to what extent changes in our wealth, in any of the six capitals, is due to unpredictables or our talent, skills, and sheer hard work.

Sometimes it's clearly pure luck. If you've inherited lots of money—or none; good looks—or not; physical strength—or weakness, etc., simply because you were born with those parents, that's luck.

Sometimes it's clearly only your effort and skill. Much of the time, it's somewhere in between, a mix of both.

Christina Bengtsson is a former world champion in precision smallbore rifle shooting, author of the superb *The Art of Focus: 10,9*, and consults on the art of focus. She is very clear in her book on how big a role the unpredictables played in her sporting career, and especially in becoming world champion. She is equally clear that by improving her focus and putting in long hours of practice every day (even sleeping at the shooting range to get in a couple of extra hours of practice before everybody else woke up) enabled her to make the most of her innate talents and the unpredictables.

The outcomes in your life and your investments are an inseparable weave of events and influences along your unique life path; an ordered sequence of unpredictables woven together by your talent, skills, and effort. And almost all of the unpredictables, the good and bad luck, don't merely add together; instead, they multiply each other. This changes everything, and explains why even small differences between the sequence of events in the lives of people with apparently identical talent, skills, etc. can lead to widely different outcomes. I will come back to this in Chapter 10

CHAPTER 2

Unpredictables

In this world, nothing is certain except death and taxes.
—Benjamin Franklin, 1789

Unpredictables are the essence of life.

Everything in your life, including your investments and enterprises, is strongly influenced by unpredictables.

We humans have become such successful apex predators in part because we are extremely good at finding the glimmers of predictability, and then acting on that prediction. Much of the time we're wrong, but we're right often enough.

The other reason behind our success is that our ancestors instinctively followed the ergodic strategies described in this book, because we're really good at seeing patterns and acting accordingly.

Of course, something that is a known unpredictable for you might be an unknown unpredictable for someone else. For example, in 2019, Covid-19 was an unknown unpredictable for most investors and entrepreneurs around the world, and so was completely missing in their planning and forecasts for 2020 to 2025.

For some, like myself and others living in China when SARS-CoV-1 arrived in 2002, it was a known unpredictable.

This chapter was sponsored by Phillipe Schmidig.

The known and unknown unpredictables can swing both ways. Sometimes they will bring you great fortune, at other times they will cost you dearly.

That they will come your way every day is the only certainty. Most are unrecognisable, many are insignificant, and a few have a large impact. And some of the largest impacts today began with an unrecognisable unpredictable in your distant past, now forgotten.

Sometimes it's possible to put in enough effort to turn an unknown unpredictable into a known unpredictable, but seldom into an accurately predictable. Usually the best you can hope for is being able to factor the unpredictable into your investment decision, where you know it can happen, but not if it will, nor when, nor how big the final impact will become.

Other unknown unpredictables are impossible to even turn into known unpredictables. Then, just as I described in *Rebuild*[6], all we can do is work with the probability distribution of known unpredictables and make some guesstimate about the unknown unpredictables.

Which takes us to the old saying: *life is just one damn thing after another.* Your life, everyone's life, is a dynamic sequence of one thing after another, connected by you, the person experiencing each event as their life.

Equally, every business is just one damn thing after another. Most of these damn things are unpredictables, and all too many are unknown unpredictables.

A business is a path of connected predictables and unpredictables, from the moment of conception, through all the key decisions, to wherever it ends. Much of what a business is, is unknowable. It's not limited to what you know it to be today, nor is it what it was yesterday, and certainly not what the business plan projects for tomorrow.

A business gets built in the actual world, as one damn thing after another, according to the dynamics of the business, forming the one path that is that business in actuality out of all of the infinitely many possible paths that that business could have been if the unpredictables had happened in a different sequence.

This is a lot like in quantum physics. The many universes theory, for example, explains quantum probability as the splitting of the universe into multiple parallel universes, one for each possibility. (Chapter 5 expands on this.)

At the moment you are about to decide to invest in your startup, or to found it, you have in front of you infinitely many equally possible paths that it could be, and no way to select, let alone control, which of those paths it will become—because of all the known, unknown, and unknowable unpredictables.

The first weakness of every business plan is not looking at a sufficiently complete range of the possible full paths in sufficient granularity to see each of the key damn things that might happen one after another.

The second weakness is that entrepreneurs and investors typically average first across a range of unpredictables to get an average growth rate and then extrapolate that average across the time horizon of the business plan. This averaging may not even be done explicitly. Averaging and then extrapolating the average ignores the granularity of each damn thing; which wouldn't be too bad, were it not for the false assumption hidden in this second weakness.

The second weakness changes everything. It makes many business plans both over-estimate the upside potential and under-estimate the downside risk. When one damn thing happens after another, the effects multiply, reinforcing each other. They do not add. When one thing happens to you it can change your whole life, including the future outcomes of things that happened far back in your past.

Everything changes depending on whether the dynamics multiply one damn thing by another or add one damn thing to another. Business and economics typically ignore the multiplicative dynamics of capital along the single path a business follows, which is a crucial weakness.

Because we have valued domination and control over our environment in the Western tradition, it's hard to work with unknowable unpredictables (and even knowable but unknown unpredictables), because their existence challenges the beliefs we have about the foundation of the success we are enjoying today. And so, the more unpredictables we have in our lives and investments, the more we try even harder to analyse, understand, predict, and control.

But in situations where patterns are no more than meaningless shapes in the clouds, whether our response delivers a beneficial or detrimental outcome has nothing to do with the pattern nor any analysis of the pattern.

Keep in mind as you read this book the wise words of Johann von Goethe:

'Woe to him who would ascribe something like reason to chance', and what J. Paul Getty said: *'In times of rapid change, experience could be your worst enemy.'*

To invest wisely requires deciding according to the actual dynamics, in sufficient granularity. Otherwise you are blind to the needless risks you are taking. It's high time to grasp the true essence of the unpredictables in business and in our investments.

CHAPTER 3

Capital Dynamics

Nothing in life is to be feared, it is only to be understood
Now is the time to understand more, so that we may fear less.
—*Marie Curie*

A business plan is a tool for predicting the future. A tool to enable today's decisions deliver your desired future outcome. For example, you are deciding what to do with your money today in order to have your money back, having grown more than inflation, in 1, 20, or 50 years time.

Founders use the tool to decide whether to invest their human capitals (e.g., time, intellectual, relationship capital) in starting a new business; leadership teams and boards use the tool to decide whether to continue; and investors use the tool to decide whether to invest in a business.

If the tool tells them that a wise decision is a no, then they may vary the parameters to see if pivoting to a different strategy or concept changes the decision to yes.

To take a good decision, you'd better use a tool that is neither inherently biased towards ungrounded optimism nor ungrounded pessimism.

There are five core elements in the conventional way of building a business plan.

1. Quantify all your knowable predictable and unpredictable financial flows: the revenues you expect to generate and the costs you need to

incur to generate that revenue.

2. Quantify all the data you have from market tests, previous years, and competition, and the global trends you're expecting, to get the best possible idea of other unpredictables.

3. Calculate your expected average growth rate by averaging over these unpredictables.

4. Then put these together in a spreadsheet to give you your predicted growth, and project the impact on your capital over, say, the next 10 years.

5. Add an upper and lower range based on a sensitivity analysis to show that you understand the consequences of your assumptions.

How close is this algorithm to what actually happens as your business progresses, given that some aspects of your growth are unpredictable? How inherently biased is it, and does it lead you to take decisions that are irrationally optimistic or pessimistic?

I use a narrow definition of a business's capital in this book. It starts with an initial investment (10,000 in the examples, in your favourite currency), no possibility of any subsequent investment, grows with a profitable sale, or shrinks by that week's costs with no sale. Think of it as a lens that focusses your attention on what matters to understand ergodicity, without any of the other elements in a typical financial analysis. It has some common ground with working capital: for example, if you have too little capital to cover your bills that week, you have to shut down completely.

Nothing would change in the conclusions if the calculations were done to represent revenue growth, by calculating each week according to the previous week's revenue, rather than our capital approach, where new revenue is proportional to the seed investment plus cumulative revenue to date.

The capital axis can equally be biomass, personal financial capital, self-esteem, or even that part of a listed company's market capital anchored in market sentiment—rising when some unpredictable story drives positive sentiment, or falling when one drives negative sentiment. Add to the word capital whatever adjective is relevant for your activity arena.

Let's take one set of parameters for this example: a 1.34% average weekly growth rate (predicted, for example, by market tests), yielding a doubling in the capital every year.

A founder would, in this case, show a business plan predicting a 100% growth per annum.

To keep things simple, in this business we only have two possible outcomes each week: a 50% likelihood of any given week's net revenue being either above average (the capital grows by 32.68%) or below average (shrink by 30.00%, as that week's liabilities are paid out).

Then add in an estimate of your sensitivity to changes in the average growth rate. Some of these changes might be due to known unpredictables, for example you know that your market research can easily be off by up to 30% either way (what is unknown is that you don't know which way, nor by how much). You then end up with a business plan predicting that your business will grow by 100% each year, with a sensitivity downside of only 70% and an upside of 130% p.a. growth.

This is shown in Figure 3.1, where you see the standard hockey stick of a company doubling in size each year for 10 years, with sensitivity lines[1].

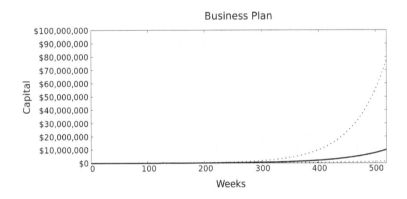

Figure 3.1: A standard business plan with a linear axis for the capital.

It's not so easy to see what is happening during the first eight years with the linear axis for the capital. So I'll plot the capital on a log axis from now on, which shows the hockey stick of multiplicative growth as a straight line. Figure 3.2 is the same as Figure 3.1 but on a log axis.

This is clearly a business that it makes financial sense to invest in.

[1] The equations used to create the diagrams in this chapter, for those who want the details, are in Chapter 7.

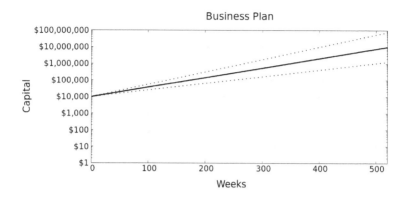

Figure 3.2: How business plans are typically calculated, this time using a logarithmic capital axis.

But is it? Well, you've already realised that I'm about to show you that it isn't, because this way of calculating business plans and taking investment decisions makes two false assumptions:

1. the specific change in the unknowables at each step in the path can be replaced by the average change in the unknowables at the start, held constant and projected out;

2. the dynamics of growth (either adding a fixed amount at each step, or multiplying the amount at the previous step by a growth factor) has a negligible impact.

Which leads to a belief that is almost always false in business: the actual path of the business will trend towards the average, we just need to keep going for long enough and the law of averages will correct for any runs of beneficial or detrimental unpredictables. This is only true when you have an ergodic system, it's false in a non-ergodic system.

Almost everything in life and business is non-ergodic, and the faster and more unpredictable the change, the bigger the difference. Business is not going to get more predictable in the next ten years.

Business school teaches us: just keep going for long enough and the law of averages will give you your annual doubling.

So it looks like a good deal for you as an investor.

This standard thinking, which expects the capital to increase, on average, week by week, with half the weeks making a little more money than the other half are losing money, is shown in Figure 3.3. This is the outcome of using the simplified statistics we're taught.

Figure 3.3: The standard way of calculating business plans assumes fluctuations trend to the average growth calculation of Figure 3.2.

Keep going long enough down the business's path and the good weeks and bad weeks will all end up converging on the expected growth rate.

If your initial forecast average growth rates are off, but still within your assumed sensitivity, then the worst case prediction is that you hit the lower sensitivity line, and the best case that you grow with the upper sensitivity line.

So let's take a look at what the same business plan predicts when we look at the granularity of the unknowables using the actual dynamics of business growth at each step. Typically business processes are multiplicative: capitals (each of the six) grow or shrink by a growth factor, a percentage of the current balance in that capital.

In this case let's look at the same 10 year business plan, as a sequence of week-to-week sales, with the same 1.34% average weekly growth rate, but now calculating correctly. Correctly means week-by-week granularity in the actual unpredictables. We use the same random 50% chance of any given week being either growth (+32.68%) or loss (-30.00%) of capital.

We are dealing here only with known unpredictables. You know what the growth rate is for the above average weeks, and the loss rate for the below average weeks. But you cannot predict which week will have growth and which week loss; nor how long you'll have runs of growth or loss.

What actually happens is shown in Figure 3.4. Clearly a losing investment, the actual growth of this business is below even the −30% range of the dotted lines, and well below the solid expected growth line.

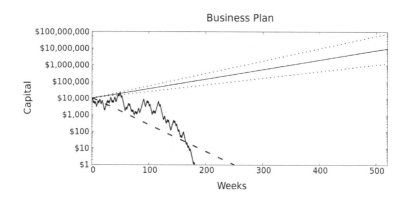

Figure 3.4: One path your business is likely to actually follow over time is shown by the heavy solid line, with collapse after 3.5 years.

Well, maybe this is the one-in-a-million fluke where the business just has a run of bad luck; too many weeks in a row of −30% losses.

In Figure 3.5 you see exactly the same business, but now I've projected the business plan into the future 50 different times, with 50 different sequences of unpredictables becoming actual and known each week. Each of these projections has exactly the same parameters, each is exactly the same business, the same business plan; the only difference is the actual growth rates each week caused by the unpredictables of that week. You can think of these as 50 different scenarios for your business, where there is nothing you can do to steer down one of them, because this is only considering the known unpredictables.

There is no way, as you craft the business plan in the present, for you to have any idea which of these projections (scenarios) your business will actually follow, if any, as it moves down its actual path for, say, the next 10 years. Both because of what you can include in your projection, the known un-

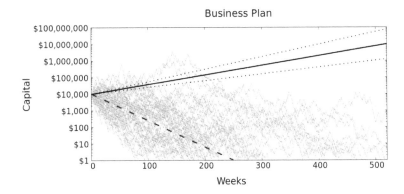

Figure 3.5: In this figure you see exactly the same business, with 50 equally possible plans projected 10 years into the future. The dashed line shows the correct expected outcome over time using the non-ergodic formula, which is always smaller than the naïve expected outcome (solid line).

predictables, and, more importantly, because of what you cannot include, the unknown and even unknowable unpredictables.

As you can see, some of these 50 plans follow your naïve business plan quite closely for the first few years. Others go bankrupt very quickly. And yet each of them is the same business with the same known unknowables in the plan, just coming in a different order, and perhaps with different numbers of up and down swings.

The expected outcome (dashed line) for your business is always significantly lower when you calculate it correctly, using non-ergodic statistics, rather than today's naïve use of ergodic statistics. The way we calculate business plans has an inherent bias towards irrational optimism. The proof is in Equations 7.8 to 7.12.

The solid line, and the dotted line sensitivity range, is using the wrong way to calculate the expected outcome. The right way gives the downward trending dashed line in the figures. Think of the simplest case: each growth event is followed by a loss event. Exactly 50-50 each fortnight, there's no variance beyond that. The solid line doubling each year uses the additive formula for the average, the false thinking commonly used; and the dashed line heading into bankruptcy in year five uses the correct multiplicative formula. (The maths is covered in more detail in chapter 7.)

The dashed line shows what happens without any runs of beneficial (good luck) or detrimental (bad luck) unpredictables.

Of course real life has far more variability, with unknowable runs of beneficial or detrimental unpredictables.

So the big message of this book to everyone using business plans: project at least 20, even better, 50 or more, individual scenarios into the future. Each scenario is drawing from the same set of known unpredictables, but in a different order and with a different number of each unpredictable across your business plan. Then take your decision to go, to pivot, or to walk away, based on the middle (expected outcome), and the best and worst in the full range of scenarios.

Only if the worst case in the range is positive is your investment clearly wise. Only if the median (middle) scenario is positive is it reasonably wise. And remember, these are all the same business, just different possible scenarios into an unknowable future.

You might be wondering what effect the fact that multiplication can be re-ordered without changing the final outcome has. Mathematically, you could put all of the growth factors into the beginning and then all of the loss factors at the end without changing the outcome.

But, and this is a big but, in actual business you cannot reorder the sequence of events and get the same outcome in all cases, because some kick you out of the game[2]. In these business plan projections, any business plan that drops as low as $1 capital is declared bankrupt at that point and ceases. In the world we actually live in, outcomes that start kicking you out of the game begin well before that, when staff leave because they lose confidence, or customers stop buying because they lose trust in the company's ability to deliver the product after payment. To say nothing of investors and banks shutting down the further investment or credit facility.

You can compare this to a casino offering you a game of business roulette. Like Russian roulette, but now with a six sided die. In this case your wealth doubles each time you throw a one through to a five; but all you have goes to the casino if you throw a six. 83% of the time you expect your wealth to double, and 17% of the time you expect to lose everything, and get kicked out of the game.

If 1000 businesses do this once, 830 can expect to double their wealth.

But if you do it 1000 times in succession, sooner or later you're out and I have everything!

The key lesson of this chapter for your investments is that a central component of neoclassical economics wisdom is false. Namely, if you have a chance to do something that is, on average, beneficial, the rational investor takes that chance. Then, if you have the opportunity to repeat that multiple times in succession, the rational investor chooses to repeat as often as possible.

The mistaken wisdom is: keep going for long enough, and eventually you will average out as a winner, which is a falsely applied 'law of averages'.

That 'wisdom' is unwise for almost all realistic business processes (in fact, for almost all processes in life) because they are non-ergodic. Only ergodic processes tend to the average expected outcome if repeated many times in succession. Non-ergodic processes *always* tend to a smaller expected outcome.

In other words, when you assume ergodicity, your calculations give you the extreme upper limit. The better your strategy is at harnessing all the inherently non-ergodic dynamics you have, the closer you can get to the ergodic limit. As you will see in this book, that means giving up hope of full control and prediction, but instead embracing the irreducible unknowability that is always part of life as a whole.

Of course, it would be equally wrong to stop doing anything to gather data, predict, and prepare for different future scenarios. In fact, now you can also use the different scenarios given by the different paths your business could take to even better predict and prepare.

As a word of warning: you could, and likely will, lie outside even these paths once the unknown and unknowable unpredictables show up in real life. The outer limits of these scenarios are not hard limits. They just tell you that the known unpredictables are unlikely to have an even worse run of detrimental unpredictables, or an even better run of beneficial unpredictables.

What is best for you depends on your nature as well. Ask yourself: "What is my true nature? Am I at heart an investor or a gambler? Am I at heart an entrepreneur, a builder of a profitable business that solves a problem or meets some need, or a builder of a Ponzi scheme that pumps money from those who joined later to the people who first got involved?"

If you are at heart an entrepreneur, one of those founders, cofounders, or members of the team living with the necessary yet irrational exuberance that you can make the impossible normal, at any given point in time you are typically committed to one business. As the much travelled story goes, you're the pig, not the chicken, in the breakfast of eggs and bacon.

So what outcome is most likely for the business that you are putting all of your time, your effort, perhaps all of your money, and maybe even the quality of your relationship with your loved ones?

Take a look at Figure 3.5: the outcome you should expect for your business is somewhere in the grey lines in this figure. The dashed line shows the median: half of the projections for your business over the next 10 years are below the median, and half above. Your business is unlikely to lie far outside the envelope between the worst and best of these 50 scenarios.

So if your essence is that of an entrepreneur building a business to solve problems and meet needs, you must get your expected outcome to be profitable. You must change what you are building until at least the middle band of projections is profitable; and ideally even the lowest band, the one with a very rare sequence of detrimental unpredictables, is at least at break even. Build according to such a strategy and you can expect to have a successful business long term, assuming, of course, that everything else is good enough: your skills, your product market fit, etc.

What if you're a gambler at heart? Then you might zero in on the first 26 weeks of Figure 3.5, where you have reasonably good odds of hitting one of the scenarios that doubles, or even one of the rare scenarios that grows 10 times in that year. Human nature being what it is, everyone, possibly even you, will then attribute that to your superior skill, rather than what it really is: the combination of your gambler's strategic choice to get out while you're winning and your pure luck in having hit a scenario with more beneficial unpredictables.

There is an intriguing intersection of gambler and entrepreneur in the professional poker player, which I'll return to on page 52. They understand the interplay between unpredictability and skill, and deploy an ergodic poker strategy to maximise their long term winnings.

Maybe you see your essence as that of an investor with a little of the gambler. Then the question is, how much money do you have to invest? You could build 50 clones of this company, where everything is identical except their exposure to external unpredictables. Then, in the first year, your fund may well be profitable averaged across all 50 clones. But, you'd better exit quickly, before even the lucky ones tend towards the dashed median line and you lose all. Because that will almost certainly happen sooner or later.

In the eggs and bacon metaphor, investors are the chickens; you can contribute to as many breakfasts as the eggs you can lay, which is why a large enough fund over a short enough time can end up with positive average returns despite falsely assuming ergodicity in their investments.

If you are primarily an investor expecting to generate a consistently positive return on investment, perhaps by the pensioners of the pension fund you are managing, you'd better make sure that you use a strategy where the expected outcomes are positive in all scenarios over the full time period.

Of course, every entrepreneur and investor also has something of the gambler, otherwise we wouldn't do what we are doing in the first place. But the better you understand what you're dealing with in the actual world, the better you will integrate intelligently both aspects of yourself into a complementary pair[6], thereby gaining even better success.

As you read the rest of the book, it is likely to dawn on you that some (many?) of the companies in each of the boom-bust cycles over the past decades were executing a business strategy with a loss-making expected outcome.

The essence of a business based on a loss-making strategy is called either a Ponzi scheme or a charity. The former is illegal and risks the founders landing in jail; and, if it's the latter, it's far better incorporated as a non-profit with donors, instead of investors expecting a return. Or as a multi-capital company[2], for example a FairShares Commons, recognising that it is net positive across human, social, or environmental capitals; and plays a vital role in enabling other businesses generate a financial profit.

Wikipedia, for example, is successful because it was never incorporated as a business. Precisely this is why so many people freely invest their time and their expertise. Were it owned and operated for financial profit it would need to pay. And the cost would likely end up beyond its means!

A business has the same essence as a Ponzi scheme if it's primarily a one-

---

[2] *Rebuild covers the range of company forms in Chapter 12*

way money pump over longer periods of time. In other words, the only thing keeping the company alive is the expectation that the stock price (or in a DAO, the crypto coin) will keep rising in value, this expectation driving a steady addition of new capital from external investors. That new capital then flows to the staff, suppliers, perhaps is used to buy customers (i.e., selling product at a loss), is channelled to early shareholders, etc.

Recall the 20 biggest IPOs[4] referred to in the preface, yielding a 42% loss compared to when they went public. Compare these to the different possible paths of a single company shown in Figure 3.5. Is this starting to look like the actual startup world? These 20 biggest IPOs are the few startups that rise, out of many. The IPO happens when they're 10, even 100 times above the target growth (solid line). Then they grow a bit more, until they eventually fall well below target.

These were the big wins in their day, yet none of them has been a star performer since. Now consider all the startups VCs invest in.

Consider that a 3× return over 10 years is the minimum needed to make sense for those investing into a fund; less than that, and they're better off investing in the public stock market, real estate, etc. A 2017 article[34] based on data from VC Gil Ben-Artzy[35] in 2016 suggests that only 5% of VC funds returned the 3× or more return to their investors, 95% underperformed, 50% so badly they lost money over the 10 year fund lifetime.

Is the message of Figure 3.5, about the difference between the actual non-ergodic capital growth in business and the ergodic assumptions we make as investors and entrepreneurs, sounding ever more like a message we must pay attention to?

The issue caused by the widespread ignorance of the difference between ergodic and non-ergodic business processes is that far too often entrepreneurs and investors think they are building a profitable business when, in reality, they are unwittingly building a loss making business. One that a purely rational stoic might label an unintended Ponzi scheme, or a charity.

CHAPTER 4

Default Strategies

*After living with their dysfunctional behavior for so many
years (a sunk cost if ever there was one), people become invested
in defending their dysfunctions rather than changing them.*
—*Marshall Goldsmith*

In the remaining chapters I write about the opportunities ergodic strategies give you for better benefitting from the result of unpredictables. In this chapter I'll touch on the default strategies, and why they fall short.

One fact is clear to every sufficiently experienced entrepreneur and investor: actual business outcomes seldom (never?) turn out the way the business plan projected. Which is why they are needed; if business was perfectly predictable, there'd be no need for entrepreneurs, nor investors, nor risk capital.

As an investor or entrepreneur, the heart of your competitive edge is your ability to deliver better outcomes, typically today by doing a better job than others of reducing downside risk and increasing upside potential. You're likely to do this by working on turning unpredictables into predictables, maximising the impact and likelihood of beneficial ones, decreasing both for detrimental ones, and contingency planning.

And so, from startups to the world's largest businesses, a body of knowledge on what to do in various business situations has been developed. However, that body of knowledge implicitly assumes that all capital-changing business processes are ergodic; but as you've just seen, they are not ergodic. And so much of that body of knowledge is, at best, a range of ad hoc patches.

This is just as true in economics; the more we grasp what the lack of ergodicity means, the more we find that these ad hoc corrections are sometimes deeply flawed and misleading. For example, what may look like irrational choices turns out to be people actually acting rationally in a non-ergodic world, as I discuss in the appendix of *Rebuild*.

Many of the default business strategies have, hidden deep inside them, the belief that there is a rational root cause for what is happening, and hence a rational strategy to deal with it. We believe that we can identify a pattern, we can predict what will happen next, if we just try hard enough and spend enough money to pin down the root cause. Then we can find the strategy to deal with the root cause.

As you have now seen, in far more cases than we realise, the root cause is inherent unpredictability. There is no pattern, there is no way of predicting what will happen next, and trying harder to find rational root causes does nothing other than haemorrhage time and money creating an illusion of understanding, control, and safety.

Once you accept that business is not ergodic, and therefore that even known unpredictables inexorably lead businesses to underperform compared to our current ways of calculating expected outcomes, you realise that some of the root causes we see are, at least in part, the consequences of non-ergodic dynamics, and cannot be addressed with our default solutions.

In a sense, you're dealing with an irrational root cause, and need something other than today's rational default strategies. I'll cover these alternate strategies in the subsequent chapters, but let's first look at today's default rational strategies.

The biggest default strategy is that of competition over collaboration. In Chapter 6 I write more about how an ergodic investment strategy delivers a context-dependent optimised balance of collaboration and competition. The right blend, you'll see, is core to thriving in a world filled with unpredictables.

By defaulting to competition, we have ended up with legislation going too far, to the point where it all too often prevents businesses from responding intelligently to their non-ergodic business dynamics. While we need some level of anti-competitive legislation, what we have today, based on the flawed assumption of ergodicity, holds us back from building businesses that can truly deliver what society and life on this planet needs.

Here are some of the other common default strategies investors and business leaders use to try to get the business to work. Of course each is absolutely a necessary part of the business playbook in our actual non-ergodic world. But unless they are used in ways fully informed by the non-ergodic nature of business they are all too often counter-productive. They actually decrease the capacity for capital preservation and capital growth, falling far short of strategies fully informed by the non-ergodic true nature of business.

Reduce headcount costs. Of course you want to reduce headcount if you truly have people filling unnecessary roles. Equally, you may well need to lay someone off if, for example, they are neither able nor willing to execute any of the current or future roles needed by the business, and cannot be retrained.

If your business growth is below the business plan projection because of the impact of a run of detrimental unpredictables, laying off staff to reduce costs is hardly strategic, because without those staff you also lack the capacity to capitalise on beneficial unpredictables when they come your way. This strategy addresses symptoms, not causes.

Young growing businesses are especially sensitive to this, because they are exposed to greater fluctuations versus their revenue. Often their headcount lags a little behind where it ought to be for the amount of work being done; but if they've experienced big funding rounds, their headcount may be running ahead. Both cases leave them vulnerable to non-ergodic growth dynamics, the middle is best.

Of course reducing headcount costs is a useful strategy when needed. Provided your fundamentals are sound, it's at least an emergency strategy to keep your core alive, in the hope that a beneficial unpredictable will arrive before too long. A bit like your body risking losing your fingers and toes by shutting off the blood supply to them when you're extremely cold. It keeps your brain and core alive for longer, but at the risk of permanently reducing your capacity.

Reduce operating costs. This is another very common strategy. Whenever you can, at a lower cost, deliver the product people want to buy, reduce your costs. Even more strategically, look at the functionality that they actually want at the price they're willing to pay for, and get to the lowest logical cost structure for that functionality.

But doing this to compensate for your business plan's mistaken assumption of ergodicity is not strategic. It's actually stumbling around in the dark hoping to get lucky.

Reduce supplier costs. Replace raw materials or components with lower-quality, lower-cost materials, in the hope that your consumers will not notice the change. Or, at least, that most of them will accept it without switching to a competing product.

We see this time and again in the food industry, for example. I (Graham) no longer buy an expensive brand of chocolate that I used to occasionally treat myself to as a student. My suspicion (confirmed by someone I know who used to be a permanent member of their tasting panels) is that they have substituted lower cost, lower quality ingredients in order to maintain profit margins.

A variant of this default strategy, if you are a big company and your supplier is small, is to negotiate their margin down. Because of the power imbalance this can often be done, even if it pushes the supplier's margins down to an unviable point leading to collapse. This has been an issue across those sectors that are the first links of supply chains, such as in farming. In chapter 9 you'll see why running and investing in an entire supply chain according to our ergodic strategy delivers better outcomes for all, including better ROI for investors.

The cost structure is always worth examining. There's no point in paying more for the supplies going into your product than needed for the functionality and experience that the consumer expects and is willing to pay for. So reducing supplier costs to an appropriate point always ought to be there; but again, it's not a viable strategy to compensate for your business plan's mistaken assumption of ergodicity, even more so because it increases the supplier's sensitivity to their mistaken assumption of ergodicity. Then the entire supply chain collapses one day, and everyone loses, including investors.

Increase product pricing (margin). Instead of reducing costs to get your actual business to match your business plan, you can simply increase your product pricing at the same cost structure.

This will always be a valid part of business. Such value-based pricing, where you charge people a price commensurate with the value that they perceive and are willing to pay for, makes sense. In some cases, certain customers actually want to pay a higher price (at least subconsciously) because what they are really buying is the personal exclusiveness, validation, or just confidence that the product is good, created by a higher price.

But this is not strategic if the reason is to patch the underlying flawed assumption of ergodicity in your business plan.

Launch a premium product. A premium product at a high price point and margin is always a strategy worth exploring. If there is a market for a premium product, and there are some consumers willing to pay that price, then launch a premium version. More often than not, not only are they willing, they want to pay a significantly higher price to have the exclusivity and reputation that are important to them.

Some startups strategically start with an aspirational product at a high price that lays the foundation for later mass-produced products at a significantly lower price with even lower total delivery costs. For example, Mercedes-Benz may first launch new technology in its Formula One car, then, as it gets the costs down a bit, put it into the high end sports cars and S-class. Some years later, Mercedes-Benz may well have developed the technology to the point that it can introduce at least 50% of the benefit at 1% of the cost into its lowest priced cars.

So this is always going to be part of the strategy playbook, but it's never a strategic way to patch the consequences of blindness to the non-ergodic nature of business in your business planning.

Pivoting. In the startup world it's very common to pivot more than once to different business concepts, which of course have completely different business plans. But what if the driver behind the need to pivot in the first place was the business plan falsely assuming ergodicity?

Then all of the investment burnt up in getting to your decision to pivot was a needlessly expensive lesson in the non-ergodicity of the actual world of business. And usually a pivot that fails to address the consequences of falsely assuming ergodicity. Another patch missing the whole point, and hence potentially even making things worse. At best just burning money in cargo cult rituals.

Whether you are an investor investing lots of money and a little of your time; or you are one of the cofounders investing lots of your time and a little money (albeit perhaps all of your money), it's far from acting with fiduciary responsibility to burn through so much capital in cargo cult rituals.

Let's look at what this means for the business projections of Chapter 3. One possible way, using a business plan based on the correct non-ergodic dynamics, to actually hit your target of doubling each year, is if the best week's growth rate increases to +37.42% and the loss in the worst week is reduced to only −25.26%.

This might not seem like much of a change from the previous +32.68% and −30.00%, but look at what it implies for the target weekly growth rate using the standard naïve equations: your interventions must increase the weekly target growth rate from 1.34% to a whopping 6.08%, or equivalently the annual naïve target growth rate goes from 100%, a somewhat realistic doubling in size each year for 10 years, to an unrealistic 2052% growth each year for 10 years.

The patches needed to deliver an actual 2× growth rate in our non-ergodic world, for the business in this specific case, require actions that would actually deliver a 22× growth rate if our assumption of ergodicity were true in the real world.

Imagine if that 22× comes from pumping in more investor money; or staff working unpaid overtime; or environmental externalities. That is a lot of capital (financial, human, and natural) that you're needlessly burning through, simply to correct for your unwitting, and flawed, assumption of ergodicity.

One analogy that came to mind illustrating the flaw of taking the average then extrapolating: imaging a farmer in the north of Germany saying "well, the coldest days of the year are at −10 °C, the warmest at +30 °C, the average is +20 °C, so my expected harvest will be at a constant temperature of +20 °C."

Then default solutions to the poor harvest, caused by running the farm according to this strategy, may be to constantly run refrigeration units on nearly half the days, and heating on the other half, chewing up significant amounts of financial and natural resources.

No wonder we are puzzled why so many good businesses, and so many good large-scale endeavours to improve business, and to harness business to improve society and our natural environment, end up falling far short of their promise. No wonder we have found it costly to build circular, net positive, regenerative economies.

Here are three examples of where, by being blind to the true non-ergodicity of business, we're making our lives hard, because of the needless wastage, across all six capitals, caused by our default strategies being unable to address the root cause.

- Net positive. Why isn't net positive the standard outcome of business? After all, everything that Paul Polman and Andrew Winston write in *Net Positive*[9] is clearly the right thing to do and ought to lead to better business results.

- Employee engagement. For five decades the Gallup polls[36] have consistently shown the range for fully engaged staff is 10 to 40%, and around the same range for the actively disengaged, i.e., those sabotaging the business.

- Job 1 versus Job 2. Kegan and Lahey[37] introduced this concept, where Job 1 is what is in your job description, and Job 2 is everything else you do in order to protect yourself and your career at work. Job 2 typically takes up more than 50% of many employees' efforts.

There is a better way, and it becomes immediately visible once we see clearly that the nature of business is far from ergodic.

This better way is an ergodic investment strategy, the class of strategies that nature has used from the start of life on this planet to thrive; despite, or better said because of, the unpredictabilities of all types and all sizes. The deeper you look the clearer it is that life has proven antifragile because the existence of unpredictables with non-ergodic capital change dynamics enables natural ecosystems to maintain their equilibrium.

Now it's time to take the next step, in Chapters 5 and 6, towards uncovering how we can do the same in business.

We will find that, the more broadly and better we execute ergodic investment strategies, the more we'll use approaches, unimaginable within today's paradigm, that work perfectly to multisolve the polycrisis we are facing.

CHAPTER 5

Science Fiction Strategies

*Cautious, careful people, always casting about to preserve
their reputations, can never effect a reform.*
—*Susan B. Anthony*

A few pages into this chapter you may say *'this is just science fiction'*. But keep in mind that good science fiction is very effective at showing us hidden truths about our reality!

The many worlds interpretation of quantum physics was first proposed in 1957 by Hugh Everett. The idea is that each time the path of a quantum particle can follow more than one path, it does, and the universe splits, leading to a parallel universe per option.

Think of the graphs of Chapter 3 in the sense of the many worlds interpretation. Then, each of the lines, each a distinct scenario that the startup could follow, actually happens in one of the parallel universes. The parallel universe that actually has that precise sequence of unpredictables.

Think of it this way: each time you create a scenario for your business, you are actually imagining a universe where this scenario happens. So comparing your business plan between multiple scenarios is the same as comparing across parallel universes as your business actually unfolds in each of the equally possible parallel universes.

So, for example, there is one universe where every single week over a 10-year period the odds are in your favour, and your startup has the best possible weekly growth rate. In the case presented in Chapter 3 your startup grows at 32.68% each week for 10 years.

Equally, there is one universe where, every single week until bankruptcy, the odds are against you, and your startup shrinks by 30% each week.

There is one universe for each possible path. So you have, every week, for 10 years, the current universe forking into two more parallel universes, where at each fork the capital either grows by 32.68% or it shrinks by 30%. Most cluster around the half grow, half shrink combination. At exactly this half-half combination, when you use the right non-ergodic equation (see equation 7.6), you get, at each step,

$$\sqrt{1.3268 \times 0.70} = 0.96372, \tag{5.1}$$

or shrinking by 3.63%. This is your most likely scenario, or expected outcome. Not the 1.34% growth the ergodic additive average predicts. This is the correct formula to calculate expected outcomes in a multiplicative non-ergodic world, not the simple average we're all taught. Chapter 7 explains the maths behind this in more detail.

So, you would be unwise as a founder to decide to start this company, or as an investor to invest in it. Even though a standard business plan tells you you should!

Your company will be somewhere off this exact sequence of one up, one down. In real business this has a significant impact. Assume it's still 50-50, but in an extreme sequence. In the universe where the company grows week on week for five years, and then shrinks week on week for five, the company will be treated very differently to the mirror universe of five years shrinking followed by five years growth.

In the latter universe the company will go bankrupt and be kicked out of the game before it ever gets to the five-year mark.

Because the order of unpredictables matters, the number of universes, i.e., scenarios, that we are dealing with here is a much bigger number than if order were irrelevant. In this example it's $2^{10 \times 52}$ or 3.43×10^{156}. That's right: 3.43 followed by 156 zeroes[1]!

---

[1] Calculated using the number of permutations of a coin with R sides, tossed N times, where order matters, given by: R^N. In our case $R = 2$ and $N = 520$. For the sharp-eyed: no bankruptcy cut-off.

Over five years, or even one year, the numbers are still huge. Five years gives 2^{260} or 1.8×10^{78}, one year is already 2^{52} or 4.5×10^{15}.

Let's play with the parallel universe fiction and see if it can tell us something that we can use to build businesses in our non-ergodic actual world.

As you read this, you may have thought *'but this isn't for me, because high variance is inherent in the kinds of highly innovative, disruptive startups that I invest in'*. By the end of Chapter 6 you will see how and why it works even better for you!

The lesson: if the universe your startup is in is the only one growing by 32.68% week on week, then the investors, founders, and everyone else will attribute that to some set of actual causes. The founders and investors will judge themselves as brilliant.

Actually the company succeeds because it struck the rarest of lucky universes having only beneficial unpredictables. It's flawed to take the success of the company as evidence that the team and investors themselves are good. That assertion is blind to their success actually coming from a one in 3.43×10^{156} lucky chance.

Quite likely, each of them will then go on to write books about how to succeed. Another book at least partly about cargo cult rituals in business.

In the universe with a startup that shrinks by 30% week on week, the investors, the staff, and especially the founders will blame themselves and everyone else for their incompetence. The investors and the founders may well end up bankrupt, judge themselves to be incompetent, and leave the entire world of startups.

Keep in mind that, in both cases, *this is the same company,* just in a universe with a different sequence of unpredictables. At the point where you create the business plan for the next 10 years, every sequence (scenario) is equally likely. The staff, the founders, and the investors are the same, there is no difference in competence between the two outcomes.

The only difference lies in the unpredictables: the order and proportion of beneficial and detrimental. And, it can get worse or better, because we are not yet including any of the unknown unpredictables in our projection, only the known unpredictables. There is absolutely no basis for any judgement on the performance of the business or competence of anybody in these examples. But because we human beings love to see patterns, and make meaning of those patterns, we falsely attribute success to competence and failure to incompetence, even in the absence of any cause-effect relationship.

Of course, once the startup actually begins moving along one path out of the infinitely many possible paths, other factors emerge, complicating the simple example we are using here to illustrate the point. For example, the investors and the founders will change their business plan, e.g. using one of the default strategies of Chapter 4, in response to a detrimental unpredictable.

Equally, if the startup moves down a path with a long run of beneficial unpredictables, investors and founders will react believing that this is their doing and take that as evidence to keep trying these default strategies in other businesses, or later on in the same business.

Sometimes all of these standard reactions to the startup growing or shrinking will be right, because these responses do address some root causes well. Just not anything caused by using the wrong equations.

It may be that the more competent team will have the edge over the less competent team as the startup progresses down a 10 year path. A more competent team may be able to keep the company going until a run of beneficial unpredictables comes. But, it may not be actual competence: what looked like competence in one company at one time and place may be detrimental in another company at another time and place, because it was actually the beneficial unpredictable causing success.

Quite clearly natural talent and learnt skills are crucial—no business will succeed without them—but the way we are taught to create business plans and interpret business outcomes blinds us to the full role of unpredictables, the non-ergodic dynamics of capital, and the best strategies to deploy.

So there are two critical questions for every investor, founder, and leader to ask.

1. How much of my success is due to a run of good luck, where the beneficial unpredictables went my way?

2. And how much is due to my skills and talent in choosing the best companies to invest in, and then shaping them?

As you have seen, beneficial and detrimental unpredictables, or good and bad luck, are far more important in success and failure than we imagine, and the dynamics driving these are not represented by the equations we are taught to use in business school. Which prevents us from seeing what is actually causing many business outcomes.

In the five books in Douglas Adams' *Hitchhiker's Guide to the Galaxy* trilogy (sic) the starship *Heart of Gold* is powered by an *Infinite Improbability Drive*. The starship makes the apparently impossible happen each time, by choosing the appropriate, but highly improbable parallel universe.

The actual strategy of VC funds today has common ground with the *Infinite Improbability Drive*. The strategy elements:

1. unicorns to deliver most of the returns;

2. have many companies at first to get a unicorn;

3. exit at the right time;

are akin to:

1. the parallel universe with the most beneficial unpredictables pays the returns to the LPs;

2. have many parallel universes;

3. exit before the unpredictables bring bankruptcy.

As you can see in Figure 3.5, showing one single company projecting its path forwards over 10 years of unpredictables in 50 different universes, there are some universes where the company grows for some initial length of time. But the number drops rapidly the greater the length of time.

If the path of the company your fund has invested in, in our actual universe, strikes it lucky because our actual universe is one of these initially lucky universes, and if you sell in time, you make a profit. But sooner or later the company is very likely to go bankrupt.

The message is clear: at least part of the investment strategy in a typical VC or PE fund (and for startup angels, and many other investment types) of today is tantamount to hoping our actual universe is one of those rare lucky universes. One[2] which gives at least one of their companies a run of beneficial unpredictables.

---

[2] Let me know if you are investing according to business plan projections calculated using correct multiplicative dynamics; in which case the above paragraph isn't applicable, and I'd love to cite you in the next edition.

A VC fund run by the character Zaphod Beeblebrox in Douglas Adams' *Hitchhiker's Guide to the Galaxy* could access all of the parallel universes for each of the companies it invests in, and average each company over all of its parallel universes (e.g., all 3.43×10^{156} universes for the company of Chapter 3). If it could break the laws of physics like that, then it would indeed get the growth calculated in typical business plans using the simplified formula.

So, in a science fiction story where the outcome of your investment in a single company is the average across all 3.43×10^{156} parallel universes that that company could follow, you do get the growth rate you predicted.

But that is just a science fiction story, you're not going to be able to do so for any actual company that you invest in.

But, what can we learn from the science fiction idea of accessing all of these parallel universes? Let's imagine we can break the laws of physics and see what happens.

Well, the one thing that you can do is invest in lots of different universes with different exposure to the sequence of unpredictables, and only invest for a very short period of time, getting out before the number of possible sequences of different unpredictables gets so big that your chances of having some universes giving you a profitable average is infinitely improbable.

Nice story, and applied in real life it leads to the successes seen by extremely large funds making large numbers of investments across a highly diversified portfolio and exiting early.

Let's imagine something close, but subtly different. What if, each week, all the parallel universes are connected together, their capitals are pooled, and then split equally across all universes?

The pure maths of chapter 7 shows that this mathematically establishes ergodicity! Now the capital dynamics are ergodic, and the company in each universe will indeed grow at the target growth rate, because the simplified, or naïve, equations you were taught to use to create business plans give the same answers as the full equations.

Close in performance—and, as you will see later, better in some ways in real life, is pooling only the profit between the parallel universes.

Figure 5.1 shows what happens applying the science fiction solution of pooling—in this case pooling all of the profit each week and sharing it out equally across all 50 universes.

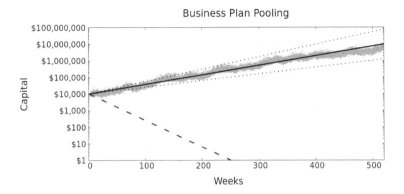

Figure 5.1: Science fiction solution with 100% profit pooling between the universes. The solid straight line is the naïve expected outcome, the dashed line the correct expected outcome, both for zero pooling.

If we pool 100% of the capital each week then we perfectly satisfy the conditions of ergodicity, and the simplified equations give the same outcome as the full equations. Pooling all of the profit each week and sharing it out equally comes close enough, as you see in the figure.

In Figure 5.2 you see what happens if, instead of pooling all the profit across the parallel universes, we instead pool 1%, 2%, 5%, and 10% of the profit. Those universes where the unpredictables lead to profit that week put a certain percentage of their profit into a pool, which is immediately shared out equally between all of the universes.

And don't forget, we are talking here about the exact same company in each universe. All of the known predictables do not change between universes, it's only the unpredictables that differentiate one universe from another.

You see that the more of the profit we share between the parallel universes, the closer the correct equations are to the simplified equation, and the more your expected outcome 10 years after founding your company approaches the ergodic maximum given by the solid line.

This pooling harnesses the full weekly variance each company experiences before pooling to reduce the capital growth variance after pooling across all of the universes. In the case where you pool all of the capital across

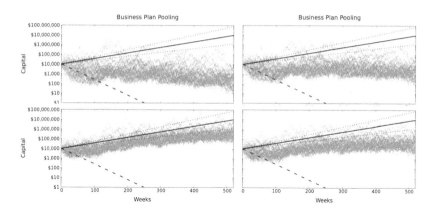

Figure 5.2: The four figures show, clockwise from the top left, 1%, 2%, 5%, and 10% profit pooling respectively.

infinitely many universes, the post-pooling variance in the capital growth drops to zero. This is the most effective way I know of to gather alpha (Nassim Taleb's quote on page vii) and preserve capital. This gives you a science fiction alpha and beta strategy!

Let's experiment with another science fiction. Imagine that you can change the laws of chance, so that your actual variance is smaller. Let's do that by adding first more possible rates while keeping the biggest and smallest the same. In this case, there is zero pooling. In Figure 5.3 you see what happens with just one more possible growth rate, exactly at the midpoint of 1.34%: reducing the variance of the week-by-week changes in the growth rate of your capital also takes the non-ergodic median closer to the ergodic maximum.

To some extent, it might be more accurate to call this a blended solution of science fiction and reality, because we can partly do this. But only for variability causes that we can predict and control.

In the actual world we live in today we have far less ability to predict and control than ever before, and certainly less than we would like to believe. So again, this is more an entertaining science fiction that may give us some ideas for what we can actually do in our real world.

Let's see what happens. The graphs have each week's capital change randomly distributed, with 50% probability of either +32.68% or −30.00%.

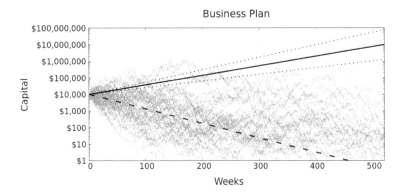

Figure 5.3: Reducing the variance by having three, rather than only two, possible growth rates in a given week. Zero profit pooling. Dashed line shows the expected outcome for non-ergodic growth with three equally probable weekly outcomes.

We can reduce the variability in two ways:
1. either smooth the steps in the probability distribution, by having more than two choices; say 3, 10, or 100 growth rates between the two extremes of +32.68% or −30.00%;

2. or reduce the extremes, keeping the same central point, for example only +3.68% or −1.00%.

As you can see, halving the gap between successive growth rates in the distribution brings your expected outcome (dashed line) using the correct equation a little bit closer to the solid ergodic upper limit line.

'*Is this Zeno's paradox*' is one question that comes up. Can we reduce the variance by taking smaller time intervals, say just one day, not one week? That doesn't help, as you can see in chapter 7. In addition, keep in mind that in real life business you have imposed time scales: short term, such as quarterly reporting and monthly salary payments; and longer term, such as changes in central bank interest rates, or the time between the next viral pandemic beginning and vaccines becoming broadly adopted. Use a time step that is meaningful for your business.

Let's look at the expected outcomes if you smooth more, comparing 2 with 3, 10, or 100 steps in the probability distribution of weekly growth rates. The change in growth rate from one week to the next can be anywhere from the lowest limit to the highest. This is not going sequentially from one rate to the next in the distribution; simply that the jumps from week to week are some of the time smaller than from one extreme to the other. You see this in Figure 5.4.

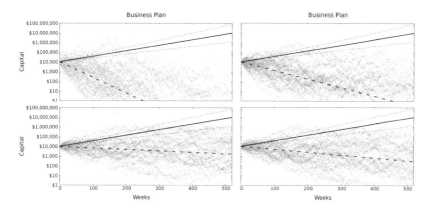

Figure 5.4: Successively smoother probability distributions. Going clockwise from the top left, starting with the original with only 2, then with 3, then with 10, and finally with 100 evenly spread growth rates in the distribution.

So science fiction is giving us another clue about how to invest successfully in our actual world, where the dynamics of business are not ergodic: reduce the actual variance in our growth rates.

As a final example we can try out in our science fiction, let's reduce the variance directly, option 2 above, by simply narrowing the distribution from the lowest to the highest.

In Figure 5.5 you see what happens if we keep to only two possible growth rates, but narrow the difference between the highest and lowest, in this figure set at either +22.68% or −20.00%, keeping the midpoint the same at the target of 1.34% weekly growth (versus the original choice of variance, +32.68% or −30.00%).

This again suggests that reducing the variance takes us closer to the ergodic limit. As you can see, the dashed line expected outcome in the actual world of non-ergodic business has lifted, coming a little bit closer to the up-

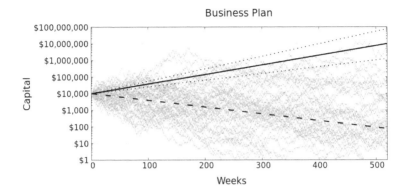

Figure 5.5: Narrowing the difference between the highest and lowest, now set at either +22.68% or −20.00%, keeping the midpoint the same at 1.34%.

per limit of a fantasy world with fully ergodic growth dynamics. It still tells you to expect to lose all your money, but it will take longer.

In Figure 5.6 you can see four different ranges between the growth week and the loss week. The closer we bring the growth rates in the worst weeks and the best weeks of your business, the closer your investment yield gets to the ergodic upper limit. Until, if they're the same, the dashed line is on top of the solid line.

This makes sense; on page 68, in the chapter on the maths, you see that the assumption of ergodicity is true if there is zero variance. This happens if your company grows by exactly the same amount every week, or in other words, there are no unpredictables.

But there's no chance of that happening in any of the companies that you invest in. Nor would it really be any fun to invest in or found a company that was even more predictable than a train on a railway track. In fact, then there is absolutely no need for any risk investment, nor even a risk loan. There's no way of gathering alpha because there is none!

And, this is fragile in the real world. It suggests exponential growth without limit, which sooner or later will break. Even if you target zero growth with zero variance it's fragile; sooner or later an unknowable unpredictable, not in your calculations, will break everything. Then you lack the vital variance to recover. Life thrives because it is superb at harnessing

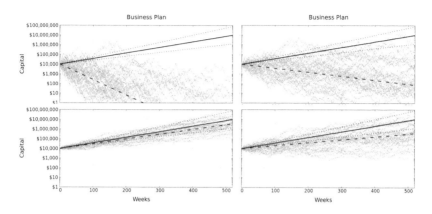

Figure 5.6: Four successively narrower differences between the highest and lowest. Clockwise around from top left, the original +32.68% or −70.00%, +22.68% or −20.00%, +12.68% or −10.00%, +7.68% or −5.00%, always keeping the midpoint the same at 1.34% naive growth rate.

variance, not because it eliminates it. How much more can you harness variance, beneficial and detrimental?

How narrow you can make the gap between weeks delivering your maximum growth and weeks delivering your minimum growth is almost entirely outside your circle of control, and to only a small extent in your circle of influence.

Now you've seen the science fiction solutions that get your business or your investment towards, or even to, the ergodic limit: either eliminate the variance in outcomes caused by unpredictables, or eliminate the unpredictables themselves over the entire time span of your investment.

But…

And this is a big but. Do it without also eliminating what makes business work. Without compromising disruptive innovation. Without bringing linear, incremental, command and control thinking into the business operations and your investment decisions. You need the variance each universe is exposed to so that you can gather lots of alpha; and gather it in a way that maximises the total you can gather over a long period of time.

And variance is always high in highly innovative, disruptive companies, with potentially very high growth rates, and very many unpredictables inherent to their business concept. The best strategies enable opposites (alpha and beta strategies) to work together as a single complementary pair[6].

So what can we learn from the science fiction solution for the actual world we live in where unpredictables play a far more important role in business performance than we like to accept?

And how can we do it at 100% on each side of the complementary pair of high and low variance; having the benefits of both? This is the ergodic investment strategy of the next chapter.

CHAPTER 6

Ergodic Strategies

Ten years ago, Peter Senge introduced the idea of the learning organization. Now he says that for big companies to change, we need to stop thinking like mechanics and to start acting like gardeners.

—*Alan M. Webber*

If you had a goose that laid golden eggs, what strategy would you follow? Would you slaughter it, slice it open, and take out the last few half-formed eggs? Or would you feed it well, and collect each egg as it came? Or would you find a gander, encourage them to 'pool their resources', then hatch the fertilised eggs, until you had a flock of geese all laying golden eggs[1]?

Likely your strategy will be: care very diligently for the goose, benefitting from the eggs it lays, while searching for a gander to scale to an entire flock, selling only the excess geese from the flock.

You'll use the slaughter strategy if you're only capable of thinking a few days into the future, or you actually face a calamity in the near future unless you get a number of days' worth of eggs now.

Yet, unfortunately, so many strategies are akin to the slaughter strategy. Individually (our health is the goose, but we don't always maintain it with a lifetime perspective); in our investments; and using natural resources (nature

---

[1] Building on a story told by Earl Nightingale.

is the goose here) faster than nature 'lays' new resources. Many countries are currently taking four to ten years' worth of resources each year.

Real fiduciary responsibility is very seldom the slaughter strategy, even if it gives a short-term illusion of responsibility.

The ergodic investor maximises, in balance, both short and long term in a world of unpredictables by embracing their true nature. They consistently deploy ergodic investment strategies, which I've named such because they leverage randomness in unpredictables to get the strategy's expectation value as close as possible to the ergodic maximum, and so outperform all other strategies' expectation values.

An ergodic investment strategy is not a case of either/or. An ergodic investment strategy may include much in existing strategies, such as the default strategies of Chapter 4, but now informed by the additional root cause of non-ergodic capital dynamics. For example, the different scenarios can give you a better idea of the range to plan for, thereby making visible a blind spot many in business have. After all, scenario planning is only as good as the scenarios an executive's imagination and beliefs allow them to see.

An ergodic investment strategy enables us to go outside the either/or forced compromise lines created by our flawed assumption of ergodicity to the whole space, such as the space of Figure 6.1 on page 56.

Ergodic investment strategies, recognising that the world of business is not ergodic, have two key foundations:

- minimise the negatives of bad luck, and especially avoid them kicking you out of the game;

- maximise the benefits of good luck.

These strategy foundations are augmented by many other cost-benefit details in the implementation, like how much is the benefit worth versus the cost of detecting and ejecting deliberate freeloaders, and actively shutting down fundamentally poor businesses.

Much as every business leader has learnt that luck is not a strategy, an ergodic investor, recognising that the business world is far from ergodic, uses an ergodic investment strategy that maximises the beneficial outcomes from all the random unpredictables across all their investees and beyond.

So perhaps the better mantra is: luck is not a strategy—except when it's ergodic!

Now let's dive deeper into how to build an explicitly ergodic strategy, one you can optimise to get maximum performance. You read in Chapter 5 the science fiction ways to achieve the ergodic maximum for a single company: connect the infinitely many copies of that company across infinitely many parallel universes, or change the physics to eliminate unpredictables.

The latter is what we've been trying without success for the past centuries: command and control to eliminate unpredictables.

In the former you deliver the impossible outcomes of simultaneously both high and low growth rate variance (this turns them from either/or opposites into a single complementary pair) by connecting the capital in the parallel universes.

Of course, in the world we actually live in, one can neither connect parallel universes nor change physics. But this science fiction of pooling clones across infinitely many fictitious parallel universes begs the question:

what if we pool capital or profit by some appropriate percentage between actual companies?

Let's look at some of the success stories we all know well, but have never before looked at through the lens of ergodic investing.

First, this is, in effect, what companies with multiple brands do: they pool, to at least some extent, their brands' capital accounts, along with their staff, suppliers, customers etc. And they use the same work processes and culture across all brands.

Apple gives a very good example of this. You can read more on page 110 about why I believe Steve Jobs grasped, at least intuitively, path-dependent non-ergodic multiplicative business dynamics.

When he returned to Apple a few years after being fired, Apple was widely regarded as a role model for dysfunctional management, and very close to collapse. One of Jobs' key innovations was realising that having separate P&L accounts for each division was dysfunctional. For example, costs in one division benefited other divisions, and significant amounts of time and money were being wasted trying to decide what percentage of these costs went into which division's P&L.

Jobs replaced this with complete resource pooling: one P&L[38] across the entire company. Immediately he began reaping the benefits of an ergodic strategy. This may well have been Jobs' greatest innovation: 100%

resource pooling in Apple.

Back then, economists and business theorists had not really begun to grasp the non-ergodic nature of business, let alone what an ergodic investment strategy is. Even today, far too few have. I suspect that Steve Jobs intuitively grasped the non-ergodic nature of business, and what to do to get close to the ergodic maximum.

This pooling of capital also showed up on 6 August 1997 when Apple was on the brink of bankruptcy. Bill Gates invested $150 million, saving the company. Yes, Gates knew that he was investing in one of his biggest competitors. But he also knew that it was far more profitable for Microsoft at the end of the day for the entire ecosystem to thrive, and for Microsoft to be part of an ecosystem much larger than Microsoft.

You read about the impact of Covid-19 on Procter and Gamble's market cap compared to the impact on Zoom and Get Your Guide on page 2.

Let's take this comparison one stage further. Imagine you're an investor, and your investment fund's strategy is focused on a wide range of digital technology solutions for tourism and hospitality. With the arrival of Covid-19 a number of those companies go under. Your fund may even collapse completely.

Even if some of the companies survive, when travel returns as Covid-19 ends and they begin performing again, your fund will be underperforming versus an ergodic investment strategy's potential.

The reason is clear: as some of the companies in your fund go under, or lay off staff, or sell assets, your portfolio as a whole loses. Many of the intangible assets your investment paid for—all of the learnings in each of the individuals, the team relationships and trust needed to deliver results efficiently and effectively—all of that dissipates.

So when travel picks up again, when the unpredictables turn travel industry growth rates positive and online meeting growth rates negative, you have to invest all that money yet again to rebuild the intangible assets you lost two years previously. It takes time before that fresh investment rebuilds the high performing team you lost. You are almost certain to fall short of the returns your limited partners (LPs) expected from your fund.

Now imagine you're an investor running a fund focused on digital meeting solutions for businesses of all sizes, like Zoom. Your portfolio takes off massively, and if you exit at just the right point, your fund massively exceeds your promised returns to your LPs, leaving the later losses, as the share price drops down again, to those that bought the shares.

Compare these two to companies like Unilever and P&G. No one had to be laid off in a hurry. The only people laid off were those who would have been laid off anyway. No hitherto healthy brands were sold in a firesale. Instead, production lines reduced their output of products selling less, and increased their output of products in high demand; and staff throughout the company, from upstream research through to frontline production and sales, were transferred to new assignments aligned with the new business context of the Covid-19 world.

Highly skilled staff, used to working within their culture, using their highly efficient standard work processes, developed new products, or rapidly added generic products. For example, nearly a dozen P&G production lines switched to manufacturing facemasks, and others turned to alcohol hand sanitizer. In Unilever, new research showed a new product benefit: its mouthwash reduced Covid-19 viral load in mouths[39], enabling it to grow the mouthwash business while others slowed.

Compare, say, P&G with a portfolio of 65 products in one single company, to a mirror private equity fund with a portfolio of 65 fully independent companies each with one product. In P&G all are rolled up into one capital pool, with a single top-level corporate capital account, workforce, culture, etc. In the PE mirror the 65 fully independent companies have no pooling, and independent capital accounts, cultures, workforces, etc.

P&G runs a different resource pooling strategy to Apple during Jobs' second stint; different brands and business units are still separate and compete with each other. So the company left some potential collaboration benefits lying on the table, in order to get the benefits of competition between its own brands. 100% pooling is not always the sweet spot in all frames of reference.

Apart from high-frequency traders, investors do not typically invest for seconds or minutes. Investors invest for some appreciable segment of a company's entire path. And that path is an ordered sequence of one unpredictable after another. So the intelligent investor, recognising that they're investing in a non-ergodic path, has a strategy to get that entire path as close as possible to the ergodic limit, from the moment of their first investment to the sale of their last share.

Not doing so is neither intelligent, nor is it acting with fiduciary responsibility.

Another example of an ergodic strategy being used without full awareness of what it is nor how to execute it with excellence: capital pooling is already practised to some extent by the limited partners of a fund. The investment fund is, even if they aren't aware of it or named it as such, an ergodic investment strategy for the limited partners. After all, what is an investment fund other than a number of individual investors pooling their capital?

Consider the alternative: each limited partner instead invests all the capital one company needs as a solo investor. No pooling, maximum risk of complete loss, and maximum chance of luck. We all know how well that works!

Instead, limited partners tend to pool their capital with many others via a fund. Even if they invest directly, perhaps as smaller angel investors, they often invest as a syndicate, which gives some of the benefits of an ergodic strategy's capital pooling.

A benefit for limited partners is the human capital pool of due diligence, especially the information and insight only one person has. This leads to a better average of good investment decisions, and hence better investment outcomes, for less time, effort, and risk.

A much more important driver of returns for these limited partners is the ergodic investment strategy implicit for them investing in such a fund.

However, for the investee companies in a typical fund's portfolio there is zero benefit. The fund investing in a portfolio is not executing an ergodic investment strategy, because nothing changes the capital dynamics of any of the portfolio companies. So the time expectation value of the fund will underperform versus the typical ensemble average return promised. Unless the member companies in the portfolio pool profit.

Successful Japanese Keiretsu, Korean Chaebol, and all of the similar business structures in Asia, perform the way they do partly because there is some level of pooling of one or more of the six capitals between diverse member companies.

You also find this in groups of cooperatives like Mondragon. In the 2008 recession, some of the companies within Mondragon closed down, and others laid off members of the workforce. None of them entered the

Spanish unemployment market because Mondragon operates its own internal social security net, i.e., a financial and human capital resource pool. Mondragon sees clearly the competitive edge it has by spending just a little money to keep, in the overall connected ecosystem, the present human capital value created by its historical investments in people: the skills in using the Mondragon way of working, and living the Mondragon culture.

> I (Graham) experienced what I would now name an implicit ergodic strategy many times while working for P&G in China. On one occasion a management team visited three suppliers working on a range of different electromechanical products. Following standard practice, every project tender would go to more than one potential supplier, and the one best fitting the selection criteria would get the project. We believed these three suppliers were pure competitors, and that pure competition would yield the best outcomes for P&G.
>
> Imagine our surprise when, in the meeting with the first supplier, the CEO midway in the meeting calmly shattered our illusion saying "by the way, company X, working on project Y, was having serious issues solving a critical technical challenge. It was on the edge of needing to delay the start of production, so I lent them a few of our engineers, and together we solved the challenge and got your project back on track".

Yes, these companies were competing with each other for our business. And they saw the bigger picture: that by making sure P&G saw China, or at least their part of Guangzhou, as the place to manufacture our electromechanical products, each would individually benefit even more. (Think it can't work in your country, and so you don't even try it out? But what if it does work better, and you don't try it, but another country does?)

So regardless of how the unpredictables affect a single business, the ecosystem as a whole retains the maximum possible value created by everything invested historically, across all capitals.

Bigger picture success (the strategy of caring for and scaling the goose) clearly requires a blend of collaboration and competition, an appropriate level of collective resource pooling and individual resource hoarding, not the 0% collaboration—100% competition strategy naïvely dictated by conventional economic dogma.

Now let's look more closely at what is in an explicit ergodic investment strategy, and what levers are at hand to optimise the strategy for each business context.

Take another look at Figure 5.2. Imagine that 50 equally competent founders have started 50 companies, each being equally good across every single metric, including product-market fit. And each is exposed to exactly the same set of unpredictable cash flows week by week, just in a different mix and order. For now take these to be the same two options, either the week's cash flow is positive +32.68% or negative −30%.

With no pooling, you know from Figure 3.5 that the expected outcome is bankruptcy after five years, and any of the lucky companies still operating after 10 years are heading towards bankruptcy. Remember, all differences are due to unpredictables; we stripped out the impact of everything else.

For the founders, this is a game they are likely to lose, sooner or later.

For the investors as well, they are likely to lose sooner or later.

Of course, for some of the entrepreneurs, in the first year or two things can look quite good. And if you are an investor, with a large enough investment fund to invest in all 50 companies as the sole investor, your average returns are healthy in the first year or two, yet start dropping the longer you hold the investment.

You see this clearly in Figure 5.2. If each of these 50 clones is being completely invested in by one investment fund, then the fund performance is given by the average return of all 50 companies. The more pooling you have between the companies directly, the better the fund's performance. And if the fund is expected to perform consistently well across decades, the more important pooling is to get healthy long-term returns. This makes clear why typical portfolio investing is a one-sided and weak attempt at ergodic investing. Unless it has partial profit pooling between the portfolio companies.

This comes back to the question we asked at the beginning of the book: what is your essence? Is your essence primarily that of an investor; or is it primarily that of a gambler? As we discussed on page 5, gamblers really only have some chance of winning without pooling if they spread their bets and quit while they're ahead.

Serious poker players have grasped this. Of those who play poker consistently, perhaps earning their living from it, some use an ergodic strategy. They compete, yes; and they use a winnings pooling mechanism to reduce the impact of unpredictables. Each member has their expected value, what they would expect to win as an ensemble average. If they win more, their excess goes into a pot; and if they win less, they receive from the pot.

This keeps all players able to play long-term, maximising the actual winnings for each individually. Each is always able to enter the next game with the capital needed, because a run of detrimental unpredictables won't prevent them from playing again. And so the long term expected outcome is now dominated by skill, not by short term unpredictables. The price willingly paid for consistent long term winnings is the short term top slice of a random improbably high win.

If ergodic strategies enable poker players to succeed, along with the other examples above, it's high time entrepreneurs began pooling between businesses, and high time their investors mandated it by only investing in entire ecosystems of businesses pooling profit.

The ergodic investor's or entrepreneur's strategy has the right amount of pooling in each of the six capitals, somewhere between 0% and 100%. Exactly where the sweet spot is depends on many factors, including many unpredictables, some even unknowables. And the sweet spot is dynamic, not stationary; it changes as the business context changes.

Finding and staying within this ever changing sweet spot is partly a technical challenge[6] guided by facts, but it's far more an adaptive challenge, i.e., one requiring changes to our beliefs and identity. Because the critical pillars concern governance in the companytocompany ecosystem (stratum 5, explained on page 76.)

A number of key pillars enable ergodic investment strategy execution.

- Trust. This is the big one. Incorporation as we know it today began four centuries ago when the amount of capital needed to start the big trading corporations, like the East India Company, exceeded the capital that one family could deploy. Up to this point, the people investing their capital to form a business trusted each other and the founder because they were family.

Incorporation solved the problem of trust between strangers by externalising trust into the incorporation systems and interactions. So that people who did not know each other—or, perhaps even, worse *did* know each other yet neither liked nor trusted each other—could still collaborate, because incorporation leads to the same outcomes that human-to-human trust would.

An ergodic investment strategy ought to use the most effective structures and interactions so that all the capitals and all the stakeholders in the pool can achieve the outcomes of trust, even if one or more stakeholder groups is seen as a traditional enemy, or inherently untrustworthy by another stakeholder group.

This is a lot like nature. Nature as a whole works extraordinarily well, with very powerful emergent governance processes, because they enable lions and tigers, antelope and rabbits, plants and fungi to each play their natural role to the fullest extent. This is what enables nature as a whole to be phenomenally antifragile, even though the nature of their individual life paths makes each individual life fragile.

- Innovation. One of the biggest drivers of innovation is an existential threat. A significant amount of progress in business, across society, and in our personal growth as human beings, is in response to a present or potential future existential threat. This means that there needs to be enough competition for the level of innovation needed for the ecosystem as a whole to thrive by adapting at the speed of change.

Again you see this in nature; evolution thrives on competition to deliver antifragility. (But in combination with collaboration, both as a complementary pair[6].)

- Weak companies. One important risk for multi-product companies is the sunk cost fallacy, such as keeping a product going because it has become the pet project a senior manager has invested their career in. Competition in the startup world (as in nature) is excellent at killing off companies with a weak product-market fit.

In an ergodic strategy with fractional profit pooling you still need effective processes to shut down weak products, but instead of blind competition you do it with targeted data-based processes to cull them, and limits on the resource pooling percentages.

- Not yet strong companies. Distinguishing between a company that is inherently weak across its path and needs to be shut down, versus a company that is strong across its path, but has not yet grown into its strength, or is experiencing a long temporary run of downward unpredictables. If it's inherently strong but looks weak now, if you do too little resource pooling or have excessively blunt mechanisms to close companies, you may well shut off the very companies that your ecosystem later requires to survive unpredictables.

- Freeloading. Similarly, key is distinguishing between actual freeloading individuals or companies, and those whose time has yet to come. Getting perfect data for these decisions costs time and money, time and money that may be more profitably invested in positive results rather than cost avoidance.

An ergodic investment strategy, recognising that unpredictables cannot be eliminated, finds an optimal balance between carrying some small percentage of freeloaders versus the time and money it takes to find out for certain. The unpredictables sometimes mean that it will take decades to tell the difference between a Van Gogh dependent on his brother's money, and a freeloader whose output will never have any value.

The last thing you want is what happened to Van Gogh: a person or business, extraordinarily valuable in the long-term future, exits the ecosystem before the value of what they were doing becomes sufficiently clear. Because no one else could see what only that genius could: the future context that required their work to begin now.

You also need to protect against those who are part of the ergodic strategy execution, but not fully committed to the ecosystem, from acting in short-term selfish interests, poisoning the well for everyone. These could include investors who are not part of your syndicate or mindset, suppliers, customers, maybe the cities the companies are in, and even national governments.

- Diversity. What kind and quantity of diversity is the minimum, and optimal, across the companies in the pool? If all the companies are affected simultaneously, and in the same way, by the same unknowables, even 100% pooling is no help. To really benefit, you need to have a sufficiently large, sufficiently diverse, and sufficiently strongly connected ecosystem of companies. One with many different short and long term countercyclical responses to a given unpredictable; and where the unpredictables cause the widest range of effects.

These pillars fall into three categories.

1. The structures that shape how wealth is generated and can flow in each of the six capitals.

2. The interactions, i.e., actual flows of each capital, and interactions between them.

3. Governance, or what decisions are made, how, and why. These are again structures and flows of the governance information.

These three categories are the three facets of an ecosystem.

As I wrote above, the sweet spot is a moving goal. Even worse, you can never have certainty at any point in time about exactly where your sweet spot is.

This reflects the fact that business today is often in the Cynefin[40] complex or chaotic quadrants[2]. A good ergodic strategy is therefore always an adaptive strategy, constantly changing at the speed of change to respond to the consequences of strategy and execution.

Avoid thinking of your sweet spot as lying somewhere on the compromise straight line in any of the dimensions or variables relevant to your businesses. Rather, you have the entire area spanned to operate in, for example the two dimensions of competition and collaboration shown in Figure 6.1.

Executing a strategy that is at the sweet spot in the entire space (for example, one that has 80% collaboration and 80% competition) is where you have a competitive edge over others. The sweet spot typically lies outside the compromise line where competition plus collaboration must add up to 100%.

I find a delicious irony in this: ergodic strategies out *compete* because they out *collaborate*!

---

[2] If you're not familiar with Dave Snowden's work, it's well worth looking at: it explains this clearly.

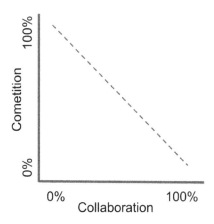

Figure 6.1: The full collaboration—competition space, or any other pair of concepts commonly seen as a polarity.

Everything in this book also applies to groups of investors and funds. Each individual fund is more likely to deliver better performance when a group of funds, forming a strongly connected ecosystem of ecosystems according to a higher order ergodic investment strategy, has an appropriate blend of collaborative pooling and competition.

You might wonder what impact fund size has. The bigger the fund is, the more likely it is (at least over short enough time spans) to outperform smaller funds for its limited partners, because the fund itself is a bigger pool of limited partners' capital. But, whilst the limited partners themselves benefit (versus investing directly in individual companies) from their executing a partially ergodic investment strategy, their returns are still lower than the potential if the fund itself executes an ergodic investment strategy, where the investee companies in are part of some form of inter-company fractional profit pooling.

If you are a relatively small angel investor doing good at the earliest stage with cheques of a few thousand only, you have a disproportionate power to do well and to do good. Only invest based on business plans using the correct equations and if the startup joins a fractional profit pooling ecosystem. Because you are in at the start, you have power to ensure an ergodic strategy is used, and to gain full benefit!

Equally, if you are an entrepreneur, never again use the naïve and irrationally optimistic way of calculating your business plan: first averaging over variability and then projecting that average.

Instead, calculate at least 50 scenarios using the correct non-ergodic formula and only go forward if enough of those are profitable. How much is enough? That's up to you, because it depends on how much of your essence is gambler! If you are primarily not, I'd say you want at least 45 of 50 projections over 10 years to be profitable, giving you only a 1 in 10 risk of random undeserved business failure.

But if you're not in a fractional profit pooling ecosystem, your expected outcome for yourself and your investors is strictly below the ergodic maximum, so you're still not acting with full fiduciary responsibility. Not to yourself, your investors, nor to any of the other capitals and stakeholders.

The more you as an individual founder, or leader of a business, build your strategy taking the non-ergodic nature of business into account, the better your performance will be, because you significantly reduce exposure to detrimental unpredictables and significantly increase your ability to fully grasp beneficial unpredictables at low cost.

So if your essence is that of an entrepreneur, make sure that the company you found is executing an ergodic strategy, by being part of a fractional profit pool with a large number of sufficiently diverse companies. Or if you are an employee looking for a stable, predictable income, join a startup in just such a fractional profit pool, or work for a larger company with a diverse range of product categories.

Then you have the best odds that all of your talents, skills, and grit will, at the end of the day, deliver success; regardless of what detrimental unpredictables are thrown at you. Because you are best positioned to take advantage of the beneficial unpredictables when they come your way. And, at the very least, by a run of detrimental unpredictables not having bankrupted you before a beneficial unpredictable arises.

The intelligent investor and entrepreneur of the future (and the future is already here, only sparsely distributed and somewhat invisible) follows an ergodic investment strategy. They invest in, or start up, strongly connected ecosystems of companies, at all scales, sitting at the sweet spot between collaboration and competition, with just the right amount of resource pooling across all capitals, at the right size, and with appropriately matched processes to create, grow, shrink, and shut down companies.

Strongly connected ecosystems (i.e., resource pooling) that are built to simultaneously deliver the complementary pair of both high and low variance in the growth rate needed to deliver the other complementary pair: both maximise the outcome of the investment and minimise downside risks threatening capital preservation.

This makes such strongly connected business ecosystems maximally antifragile, enabling maximally successful investing in high potential growth, disruptively innovative companies. Exactly the kind of companies needed today to solve our global climate, social, and biosphere problems.

Use the strategy that nature uses, and build the way that nature builds.

The next step is crafting and executing an ergodic investment strategy with full understanding. This can best be done with an ecosystem of profit or capital pooling businesses, appropriate to your business in size, diversity, and governance.

CHAPTER 7

The Mathematics

*The Universe […] cannot be understood unless one first
learns to comprehend the language and interpret the
characters in which it is written. It is written in the language
of mathematics, and its characters are triangles, circles, and
other geometrical figures, without which it is humanly
impossible to understand a single word of it; without these,
one is wandering around in a dark labyrinth.*
—*Galileo Galilei, in* The Assayer

Here I give the mathematics, the language of the non-ergodic nature of
capital processes, to talk about the practical application of this book: how
to build strategies and businesses that thrive in a world filled with such non-
ergodic capital processes.

If you are only interested in what to do to benefit from these insights
into how the world of business actually works, just skim the text between
the equations for whatever is valuable to you. That's enough.

The equations themselves are hard work, unless you've an advanced
maths or physics background; but if you have that background, you may
want even more detail. Go to our Evolutesix website, and read the original
research papers on ergodicity economics. Start with the most recent and
relevant from Peters and Adamou[41], then the first paper from Peters and
Nobel laureat theoretical physicist Gell-Mann[42], as well as these papers of

Peters and collaborators[43–45]. Keen's *The New Economics*[46] and Wilson's *This view of life, Completing the Darwinian revolution*[47] provide relevant underpinning from an economist's and evolutionary biologist's perspectives.

Everything in this chapter is just mathematics describing how things change over time. It doesn't care what you want the world to be.

Unless you use the maths that describes the actual world, you are describing an imaginary world. If you want to invest in, start, or lead a fundamentally successful business in the actual world, you have the best chance of success if you're using the maths of the actual world.

Let's start by defining what ergodicity means. In any process with randomness, there are two ways of figuring out what to expect in the limit where all the randomness cancels itself out. Either you let time go to infinity in one system, or you average over infinitely many systems at a fixed time. If these two ways give the same answer the system is ergodic. But often the path matters, and the two answers are different. The system is non-ergodic.

Now the mathematical illustration. Let's say that you have some variable x (for example, your capital balance, for any capital, including biomass) that can have, at any point in time, one of the values out of a set of all possible values for x. This set of all possible values is called the ensemble. Then the expected value $\langle x \rangle$ of x is the arithmetic (add them) average (divide by the total number of values) of all values of x in the ensemble. This expectation value of x is called the ensemble average, the arithmetic mean, or just the average:

$$\langle x \rangle = \frac{1}{N} \sum_{i=1}^{N} x_i \qquad (7.1)$$

for an ensemble containing N possible values for x.

There is a second way of calculating the average if you're looking at a sequence on a path you've travelled along for some length of time. In this, the time average, we are looking at a sequence of the variable x over time, and taking the average across time from the start to the end of the sequence:

$$\bar{x} = \frac{1}{T} \sum_{t=1}^{T} x(t) \qquad (7.2)$$

where each of the $x(t)$ are taken from the same ensemble with N possible values for $x(t)$.

The ensemble average is calculated at a specific point in time across the entire ensemble, and the time average is calculated across time on a specific path. If these two are equal, $\bar{x} = \langle x \rangle$ for a large enough period of time, (strictly speaking, infinitely long) then we say that the dynamics are ergodic. If these are not equal, $\bar{x} \neq \langle x \rangle$, then we say that the dynamics are non-ergodic.

Recall the chessboard example I introduced in the preface, on Page viii, illustrating with one simplistic example, the difference between the path or time expected outcome and the average.

If 10,000 people play the game once each, the total change to the bank accounts will be $10,000\langle x \rangle$. If you play the game, walking at random from square to square, according to the fall of your dice, for 10,000 steps in sequence, your expected outcome is $10,000\bar{x}$.

In the preface I made even more clear the role of the path's dynamics by limiting the allowed moves. Now you can see that even if the dynamics allowed you to move to all squares the expected outcome along the path is still different to the average.

This example of ergodic thinking shines a powerful light on one of the myths in economics harming business and investment today: the myth that if an opportunity is beneficial on average once, and you have a chance to repeat it, then it is beneficial to repeat it. Ergodic thinking also makes clear that another core belief is a myth: that competition is the default strategy for individuals winning and needs no explanation, collaboration needs a behavioural explanation. Ergodic thinking shows that collaboration, fractional profit pooling, is the default strategy, pure competition needs an explanation.

So why have we been using the wrong maths for so long? The time average is typically much harder to calculate than the ensemble average. Sometimes it's impossible to calculate with any closed equation; then, all you can do is a brute force simulation by computer to get some idea of what to expect.

The path dependent time expected outcome is what matters in business, because business is a sequence of one thing after another along one path. If you want to decide to invest in or found a startup, based on whether or not the most likely outcome is a healthy future return on investment, you need the time expectation for how money changes.

What you need to know, to take that investment decision, is the median, or middle outcome. The median outcome is the watershed where half the outcomes are better, and half are worse. And if, say, 90% of the range of outcomes around the median are profitable, you decide to take the risk of investing in or starting up the business. (Sometimes the mode, the most common outcome, might also be useful. I'll leave that for another book.)

Typical business plans use the ensemble average growth, not the correct time expectation, because few are aware of the capital dynamics, and the difference between ergodic and non-ergodic dynamics.

This is equally the case throughout economics; only within the past decade have leading economists begun to realise that most of the capital processes in the economy are non-ergodic.

The bigger and faster the volatility, the bigger the gap between the correctly calculated time expectation and the naïve calculation based on the ensemble average. And as you'll see below, for capital growth processes the time expectation is always smaller than the naïve expectation.

Until recently, most people crafting business plans used the ensemble average to tell them what to expect from their business in the future. The ensemble average can only tell you about the future of your business if your capital processes are ergodic. But capital invariably has non-ergodic dynamics, except in the rare case that they are constant across time. Not something that you find anywhere in life, including business!

So given that your capital is changing over time, your focus as an investor or business leader is to take decisions today by predicting what you can expect the capital you invest will become in the future; especially the risks of it being less than that, or even lost entirely.

You only invest if you expect it to grow by enough to counterbalance the risk of losing it. Otherwise, if the most likely outcome is losing part or all of it, you're a philanthropist donating to a worthy cause; or, perhaps better put, you're investing financial capital in order to grow social or natural capital.

Unlike the first two equations for purely additive processes, which I used as a simpler illustration of ergodic versus non-ergodic dynamics, capital typically grows multiplicatively (it grows by a percentage of the current value). This makes the maths even more complicated, and is one reason why most use (incorrectly) the ensemble average.

To calculate the expected growth rate of some capital $C(t)$ at a time $t = T$ we've been taught to start with the ensemble average growth rate over all the known unpredictables, given by equation 7.3:

$$\langle g^{\mathrm{a}} \rangle = \frac{1}{N} \sum_{i=1}^{N} g_i \tag{7.3}$$

where $\langle g^{\mathrm{a}} \rangle$ is the ensemble average growth rate of $C(t)$ per time step Δt, with N possible individual changes to the capital, each possible change is given by g_i and each is equally likely to happen. In other words, it's known what kind of things can happen, and certain that one of these happens each time period; but unpredictable exactly which will happen when.

Each of the g_i can be positive or negative: a beneficial or detrimental unpredictable.

And so your expected capital growth after some length of time T (measured in units of the time step Δt) is given by equation 7.4:

$$\langle C(T) \rangle = C(0) T \langle g^{\mathrm{a}} \rangle \tag{7.4}$$

where $C(0)$ is your starting capital, $C(T)$ is your capital at some later time $t = T$, after having grown at the arithmetic average growth rate $\langle g^{\mathrm{a}} \rangle$, and $\langle C(T) \rangle$ is final capital you are most likely to have.

Typically an entrepreneur will set, or have set for them by their investors, some target growth rate; let's call that target growth rate μ. The entrepreneur can only influence whether their expected growth rate from the ensemble of unpredictables equals the target ($\langle g^{\mathrm{a}} \rangle = \mu$) by varying their cost structure and their margin. So the entrepreneur will look at all of the default strategies, such as in Chapter 4, exploring different combinations in a spreadsheet, until they find a combination where the ensemble average hits the target μ.

This is what we are all taught, and is to be found across the texts used in business schools and economics courses, and in almost all business plans. But it's not valid. The ensemble average growth rate $\langle g^{\mathrm{a}} \rangle$ is not a good predictor of the business being able to achieve the target μ at some future time T.

Some common equations used in economics and in business today are only valid for ergodic capital growth dynamics. Their use began in physics and mathematics, and were reapplied in economics nearly four centuries ago. Then, late in the 19th century, after economics had disconnected from physics, physicists learnt that the dynamics of certain physical processes were non-ergodic, and knuckled down to the hard work of using the correct general case equations applicable to both ergodic and non-ergodic dynamics.

Leading economists now realise that the specific dynamics of economic change processes cannot be neglected, and that these seldom have ergodic dynamics. Innovative entrepreneurs are now also picking up on the implications of this for being successful in business.

The reason the simple ensemble average fails to tell us what we need to know about the future of a business is that, not only does each business follow a path across time, a sequence of events changing the capital, but most capital growth processes are not additive. Instead, they are a sequence of multiplications along a path (e.g. compound interest) where the order of the sequence matters. As discussed in Chapter 3, this gives different outcomes to those predicted using the ensemble average, at times significantly different.

To calculate correctly the future outcome in such a case you need to look at predictions of the kinds of paths that are likely to actually happen. Equation 7.5 is the one I used to calculate the individual path in Figure 3.4 and each of the individual paths in subsequent figures showing multiple scenarios for the same business.

$$C_j(T) = C(0) \prod_{t=1}^{T} g_j(t) \qquad (7.5)$$

In these equations $C_j(T)$ is the capital balance along path j at time T, where $g_j(t)$ is the actual growth rate (positive or negative) in week t along path j. In other words, $g_j(t)$ is the actual unpredictable that happens in the business scenario j at time step t from the ensemble of all the possible unpredictables at that time.

The order of unpredictables in the sequence is important here: in business, as in all of nature, there are situations where just one more detrimental unpredictable takes you out of the game permanently, e.g., the business goes bankrupt. Whether that happens in the 25th week or in the 2,500th week makes a difference to the investor and entrepreneur (in the 25th week, you almost certainly lose all your money; in the 2,500th week you may well have sold your shares at a profit).

So what is the expected growth rate, which is the growth rate of the median of the C_j at each time step, when the path and the order of the unpredictables in the sequence actually matter? The ensemble average gives the wrong answer, but how wrong is it, and in which direction does it mislead you?

There are two distinct expectations. One is the expected outcome if you have infinitely many identical companies that you invest in (see Chapter 5), then what matters is the average outcome over all companies. This is the ensemble average. The second is the expected outcome if you only have one company that keeps going for a long time. The expected outcome is then the time expectation. The time expectation is the answer we need if we want to predict the expected outcome of our investment in a company, because we're asking the question *'if the company keeps going at least until after I exit, will the beneficial unpredictables outweigh the detrimental ones by enough to deliver positive ROI?'*

Look again at Equation 7.4, the formula you probably use to predict what your future capital is likely to be at time T, incorrectly uses the ensemble average growth rate. All we need to do, to get a useful prediction, is replace the ensemble average growth rate with the time expectation growth rate. Looking at Equation 7.5 you can might intuitively recognise why this is the correct formula:

$$\bar{g} = \sqrt[N]{\prod_{i=1}^{N} g_i} \tag{7.6}$$

where $\bar{g}$ is the time expected growth rate, also called the geometric mean growth rate.

So your expected capital at time T, which I will write now as $\bar{C}(T)$ to avoid confusion with the $\langle C(T) \rangle$ of Equation 7.4, will have grown by $T\bar{g}$, not $T\langle g^{\mathrm{a}} \rangle$:

$$\bar{C}(T) = C(0)T\bar{g} \tag{7.7}$$

Now comes the mathematical reason why this makes all the difference. If you multiply N different numbers and then take the Nth root (geometric mean) you will always get a smaller number, or at best equal, than if you add all N and divide by N (arithmetic mean):

$$\bar{g} \leq \langle g^{\mathrm{a}} \rangle \tag{7.8}$$

They're only equal if the dynamics are ergodic. So, only if the dynamics of a capital change process are truly ergodic can you use the simple calculation of $\langle g^{\mathrm{a}} \rangle$ in place of the tough calculation of $\bar{g}$.

The path-dependent multiplicative dynamics (non-ergodic), resulting in $\bar{C}(T)$ always being less than the $\langle C(T) \rangle$ prediction from falsely assuming business is ergodic, is one of the currently unseen root causes at the heart of why so many businesses end up losing the capital invested, even though the plans looked like good investments.

And part of why we are needlessly burning up natural and all of the human capitals at a life-threatening rate.

You can see why it's less with this simple example. If the dynamics of your capital growth processes are additive and ergodic, then the expectation value of the change after one step is the arithmetic average:

$$\langle g^{\mathrm{a}} \rangle = \frac{1}{N} \sum_{i=1}^{N} g_i \tag{7.9}$$

In the simple business plan shown in Figure 3.2 you only have two possible changes: grow by 32.68% (1.3268 growth rate) or shrink by 30.00% (0.7000 growth rate).

Were the business to have additive ergodic dynamics then the expected outcome is:

$$\langle g^{\mathrm{a}} \rangle = \frac{1.3268 + 0.7000}{2} = 1.0134, \tag{7.10}$$

giving a weekly capital growth of 1.34%, or doubling every year. If this is your target growth rate μ, this formula, as economists and business students have sadly been taught for a very long time[42], tells you to expect to eventually hit your target if you keep going long enough.

But if the capital growth dynamics are multiplicative, which they usually are, this is the wrong formula to use. Instead, the expected change after one step is calculated by Equation 7.6. Now you get the correct expected growth in the capital for each time step along the path when you have multiplicative dynamics, also known as geometric Brownian motion. This is shown in Figure 3.2 as the dashed line, giving the expected change in the weekly capital for our example:

$$\bar{g} = \sqrt[2]{1.3268 \times 0.7000} = 0.9637, \qquad (7.11)$$

resulting in a most likely *loss* of 3.63% per week, and eventual bankruptcy. Of course, over a short enough time period, you may have a run of good luck and hit, or even exceed, your target μ.

Clearly 0.9637 is smaller than 1.134, as you saw in the graphs in Chapter 3. If you use maths that describes the actual world we live in, you do not invest in this company, you do not start up this company, unless you see this as philanthropy, using money to grow non-financial capitals. (And you'd better use the right equation for those capitals as well, or risk decreasing all of the capitals you touch!)

It's worth stressing: the geometric mean is always smaller than the arithmetic mean, so a business plan using the arithmetic mean or ensemble average is always even more biased towards irrational exuberance than you already know.

Except in one unlikely case: if all the numbers going into the mean are identical. In other words, there is absolutely no variance at all in the dynamics of your capital processes. Every second, every minute, every week, every year is identical to every other.

So now you know the answer to the first part of the question above, in which direction does incorrectly using the ensemble average to predict the future of the business you are starting, or investing in mislead you: it always biases you towards ungrounded optimism. Now, the question is, by how much?

The simplest case is if all of the possible changes in the capital g_i come from a time independent normal distribution. For geometric Brownian motion these g_i have an expected value

$$\bar{g} = \langle g^a \rangle - \frac{\sigma^2}{2} \qquad (7.12)$$

which is $\sigma^2/2$ smaller than the arithmetic mean. This gives an expected loss, not growth, if $\sigma^2/2$ is bigger than $\langle g^a \rangle$. σ is the standard deviation of the normal distribution of the $g_i(t)$.

In other words, your expected outcome, when you keep going, is simply not going to *'trend towards the mean'*, if you mean the ensemble or arithmetic mean $\langle g^a \rangle$.

Clearly, the smaller that you can make $\sigma^2/2$, the more likely it is that your business will be successful. If you can reduce to zero the variability that your business is subject to, then you lift your expected growth up to what I am calling the *ergodic maximum*, the arithmetic mean. A business typically builds itself to deliver an arithmetic mean equal to or greater than the target growth rate μ.

Which now takes us into the next set of equations used in Chapters 5 and 6 to illustrate the central message of this book: why every single business is best able to succeed for itself if it pools capital with other businesses.

This pooling of capital is described by the following equations. First, the change in the capital $C_j(t)$ of company along path j at time t is

$$\Delta C_j(t) = C_j(t)(\mu \Delta t + \sigma \xi_j(t) \sqrt{\Delta t}) \qquad (7.13)$$

where μ is your target capital growth rate that you would hit ($\mu = \langle g^a \rangle$) if your business processes were ergodic.

This is now a more useful way of writing Equation 7.5:

$$\Delta C_j(t) = C_j(t) g_j(t) - C_j(t) \qquad (7.14)$$

where $g_j(t) = (\mu \Delta t + \sigma \xi_j(t) \sqrt{\Delta t})$. The ξ are from an independent normal distribution with a standard deviation of 1. By multiplying it by σ as a scaling factor we get back our original ensemble with ensemble average μ and standard deviation σ. So

$$C_j(t + \Delta t) = C_j(t) + \Delta C_j(t). \qquad (7.15)$$

In the graphs given in this book, we plot everything using the week as the time unit so $\Delta t = 1$. This makes for simplicity, but if you need to mix different dynamics having different scales, you will need to keep time in explicitly.

With pooling there is now an extra step before going forward one time step along each scenario. We need to pool and then divide the pool out.

You can choose to pool the capital, to pool the changing capital, or to pool only the positive changes in capital, in other words the profit. In the other chapters of this book I choose to pool the profit, not all of the capital, because of a number of practical benefits in making pooling work in real life.

And for each of these, you can choose to pool any fraction from none to all of it; and you can choose to have the same fraction or different fractions for each company and / or time step. You can choose to share the pool out equally to all collaborators, or differentiate according to some criterion; and maybe subtract from the pool some amount to cover the pool's operating expenses. For simplicity of explanation, I have no deduction for operating expenses, and equal sharing.

The strongest effect, with the easiest to understand equations, comes with perfect collaboration, i.e., pooling all the capital, or all the changing capital.

High levels of collaboration exist throughout nature, including in business. For example, you're intelligent because each individual brain cell collaborates with the others. Or, a well-run business unit pools as near as possible 100% of its financial, intellectual, human etc., capitals to have the best chance of success.

So let's start with 100% collaboration. You now have, for N collaborators in the pool, at the beginning of each time step, each of the j collaborators having the same capital C^N, $C_j(t) = C^N(t)$. However the initial change in capital is different due to the fluctuations caused by different unpredictables:

$$\Delta C_j(t) = C^N(t)(\mu\Delta t + \sigma\xi_j(t)\sqrt{\Delta t}), \qquad (7.16)$$

so now each collaborator has changed its capital before pooling to:

$$C^N(t) + C^N(t)(\mu\Delta t + \sigma\xi_j(t)\sqrt{\Delta t}). \qquad (7.17)$$

But at the last moment before the end of the time period t, the capitals are pooled and immediately shared out equally, so now each of the $C_j(t + \Delta t) = C^N(t + \Delta t)$ is:

$$C^N(t+\Delta t) = \frac{1}{N}\sum_{j=1}^{N}\left(C^N(t) + C^N(t)\left(\mu\Delta t + \sigma\xi_j(t)\sqrt{\Delta t}\right)\right)$$

(7.18)

$$= C^N(t)\left(1 + \mu\Delta t + \frac{1}{N}\sum_{j=1}^{N}\sigma\xi_j(t)\sqrt{\Delta t}\right). \quad (7.19)$$

The impact of the unpredictables has been reduced by a factor $1/N$, and if N is big enough, your capital will now grow steadily at the target μ.

Because maths is magic, adding up normal variates $\xi_j(t)$ gives another normal variate; so you get a new normal variate $\xi^N(t)$ for all N cooperators

$$\xi^N(t) = \frac{1}{\sqrt{N}}\sum_{j=1}^{N}\xi_j(t) \quad (7.20)$$

Which means that the new standard deviation of the cooperators together is $\sigma/\sqrt{N}$, giving you a median growth rate for N perfect cooperators $\bar{g}^N$ (cf. Equation 7.12) of:

$$\bar{g}^N = \mu - \frac{\sigma^2}{2N} \quad (7.21)$$

which clearly trends to your target μ the larger the pool of collaborators, even though your variance caused by all the unpredictables remains constant. This is why nature can be so antifragile: nature loves the kind of high variance capable of giving the benefits of a high growth trend μ across a wide range of contexts, and then uses collaboration to eliminate the downsides! And competition to prevent unconstrained growth. All together gives you an antifragile ecosystem in a dynamic equilibrium according to the changing frame of reference.

Equation 7.19 also shows that you get the same result whether you pool the capital or the changes in capital. This means in practice sharing out equally the gains of the randomly lucky, and losses of the randomly unlucky, to all collaborators.

But that's impractical in real business for financial capital, unless the different companies have as tight a relationship as the different business units in Unilever.

What is practical is sharing some fraction ρ (a number from 0 to 1) of the changes in capital, i.e., the profits and losses. I denote a positive change in capital (profit) with $\Delta^+ C_j(t)$, a negative change (loss) with $\Delta^- C_j(t)$, and no change with $\Delta^0 C_j(t)$.

But now, as capitals are pooled at the end of the time period t, the capital pool $P(t)$ at the end of each time step t has two meaningful components, the pooled profits and the pooled losses (compare with Equation 7.19):

$$P^+(t) = \sum_{i=1}^{N^+(t)} \rho \Delta^+ C_j(t) \qquad (7.22)$$

$$P^-(t) = \sum_{i=1}^{N^-(t)} \rho \Delta^- C_j(t) \qquad (7.23)$$

where there are $N^+(t)$ collaborators with total profit $P^+(t)$, $N^-(t)$ with losses $P^-(t)$ at time t, and $N^0(t)$ with no change.

$$N^+(t) + N^-(t) + N^0(t) = N \qquad (7.24)$$

Each of these pools is then divided out equally: each cooperator receives the same $1/N$ fraction of the pool $P^+(t)$ of gains, and $1/N$ fraction of the pool $P^-(t)$ of the losses.

If $\rho = 1$ there is perfect collaboration, each sharing all of the capital change, and you are back to Equation 7.19, with the time expectation growth of each company getting closer to the target μ the larger $\sqrt{N}$ becomes, as per Equation 7.21.

Equally, if $\rho = 0$, there is no collaboration, and you are back to Equation 7.5 or 7.15. The time expectation growth of each path $\bar{g}$ is reduced from the target μ by the full $\sigma^2/2$

If ρ is between these two limits, you have some of the $\sqrt{N}$ getting you closer to your target μ, but not all.

Even this equal sharing of profit and loss may be tricky to implement in practice. What can be most easily implemented is just profit sharing without any loss sharing. Investors and entrepreneurs already know this: if the company makes a profit, some of the profit is shared out to the collaborators (investors, staff, etc.) as dividends, bonuses, etc. Now extend the concept to broader criteria for membership of the profit sharing pool.

Let's define the profit $p_j(t)$ of each path at time t as

$$p_j(t) = \Delta^+ C_j(t) \quad \text{if greater than zero, or} \tag{7.25}$$
$$p_j(t) = 0 \quad \text{if } \Delta C_j(t) \text{ is less than or equal to zero.} \tag{7.26}$$

Then the profit pool at each step is

$$P(t) = \sum_{i=1}^{N} \rho p_j(t) \tag{7.27}$$

where $P(t)$ is the total pool across all parallel universe paths (in Chapter 5) or across all companies in the ecosystem (in Chapter 6). Then you divide the pool back out again. If you divide the pool equally across each parallel universe or company in the ecosystem, then each gets $P(t)/N$.

So at the end of time step t the change in capital for each path or company j is

$$C_j(t + \Delta t) = C(t) + \Delta C_j(t) - \rho p_j(T) + \frac{P(t)}{N}. \tag{7.28}$$

Keep in mind that if $\Delta C_j(t)$ is negative or zero then $\rho p_j(T)$ is zero, so nothing is subtracted from the capital, and $P(t)/N$ is added, making the net change to the capital on that path, i.e., company, positive. Vice versa, if the path or company does make a profit at that time step, then an amount $\Delta^+ C_j(t) - \rho p_j(T) + P(t)/N$, which is always smaller than the $\rho p_j(T)$ put into the pool, is added back.

So what's the benefit, and how does it work? In brief, while this looks like a loss when you only use the ensemble average to predict future performance, as soon as you use the correct time expectation to predict the future you see that this benefits each path or company individually, and all of them collectively, because it takes the time expectation (your median expected outcome) closer to the ergodic maximum, i.e., the ensemble or target growth rate μ.

This is about hitting your profitability metrics without needing to increase your prices or your costs down below the business appropriate healthy point, in a blind reaction to the consequences of your business plan biasing you towards irrational optimism.

The key take-away from this chapter is that the larger the pool of collaborators, and the more of their capital changes they pool, the better the expected performance over time of each one, if all that matters are the unpredictables.

But, of course, in real business, as in real life, there are many more factors at play. The sweet spot for actual individual companies is somewhere in the middle: an adaptive blend of collaboration and competition.

While everything in this book is pure maths, and this pure maths makes clear that resource pooling is a winning strategy, it can only work if the different parties are disincentivised from eating each other, taking the money and running, or some other action that shuts down pooling.

For people this means developing our capacity, systems, and interactions for collaborating and competing with individuals, types of stakeholders, organisations, and other companies, regardless of whether you agree with, like, and trust them; or disagree with, dislike, and distrust[7,48].

You still have a lot of space to optimise your unique ergodic strategy. You can freely choose how big ρ is, if it changes over time, or differs for different kinds of pool members, what the criteria are for gaining or losing membership, how and when to shut down companies with weak fundamentals, as well as all of the business strategies you are already using.

CHAPTER 8

Building Ergodically

Knowing is not enough, we must apply. Willing is not enough, we must do.

—*Johann von Goethe*

Having decided to follow an ergodic investment strategy, the next question is how you can build and operate companies accordingly. Many factors can be addressed. Which ones you would benefit from addressing in your investments or companies is part of the skillset and intuition you will build by designing and executing your own ergodic investment strategy.

The way we build business today is very much about building for predictability, despite the true nature of business being dominated by unpredictables. It's time to stop wasting capital, and start building in full positive complicity[1] with the unpredictable non-ergodic essence of business.

Building for non-ergodic unpredictables doesn't mean that we completely roll over and give up gathering data, predicting, and planning. It requires us to still do well in predicting scenarios and controlling those aspects of business that are predictable and controllable. Building for ergodicity requires integrating the contradictory opposites of predictables and unpredictables into one single complementary pair, yielding a powerful tool

---

[1] I mean here a very positive meaning, none of the nefarious meaning. Thanks to Patrick Martel for introducing us to this!

for success.

The greater your capacity to hold contradictory perspectives simultaneously, the better your ergodic strategy will be. (More on this in *Rebuild*[6].)

Even more so than in the previous chapters, every time you find yourself thinking *'but that's just wrong'*, please suspend judgement until you finish this book and have tried some things out.

Purpose is the foundation in building according to an ergodic investment strategy. But, as I write in *Rebuild* about the purpose problem, a company's purpose is an internal choice about which answer to give to an external question, or driver. What matters more is the driver, which is the external context and need. An ergodic strategy must be anchored in the driver, otherwise it will suffer from the purpose problem: not changing when the original external driver that led to choosing this specific internal purpose has changed.

So to build companies worth investing in according to an ergodic investment strategy, the starting point is a driver statement[49], the connection between the current external context and need, and your company. The driver statement is a description of what's happening and what is, in the actual world, along with one or more needs. Then it's very clear and easy to see if what actually *is* changes due to some unpredictable, meaning that it's time for the business to pivot and change its purpose. This is what enables you to recognise when unpredictables have come your way, and it's time for a major change of strategy. Maybe to tap into benefits; or maybe to leave the company you founded, or shut it down. Many of the founder's dilemmas[50] exist because it's hard to navigate unpredictable complexity.

Nokia, Kodak, and many others all failed because they were narrowly focused on an ossified purpose responding to a vanishing context and need. By only seeing the response, and mistaking that for the reason the company exists, they were unable to see how the world was changing. Kodak could not see the unpredictables happening all around them, unpredictables calling a completely new kind of image capture, storage, and reproduction business into life, and killing off the old business.

A business executing an ergodic investment strategy starts by anchoring the incorporation in the current context and needs—those you are able to see and then choose to meet. The purpose is then a somewhat trivial restatement, as the response to the driver statement.

To respond to a driver in a non-ergodic world requires an ecosystem of fractional profit pooling companies. An ecosystem has two distinct elements, inseparably woven into one: the structures or systems, and the interactions or flows. These include one critical element for business: the governance of the two elements.

In building a working ecosystem of such companies it's vital to distinguish cleanly between structures and interactions. All too many conflate them, focusing either on the structures or on the interactions.

By conflating one into the other you risk building a statue that breaks when you load it (if you conflate interactions into structures) or a shapeless gel impervious to strategy (if you conflate all structures into interactions).

You can picture what errors in judgement this creates if you think of a river. The riverbed is the structure, the water is the interaction. The actual dynamics of the river depend equally on each; a given riverbed during a drought, carrying a fraction of its normal capacity, leads to a very different river to the same bed during a once-in-a-millenium flood, with 50 times its normal volume.

It's helpful to distinguish between six different types of ecosystem, all of which are relevant to executing an ergodic strategy. Each of these is a holon: complete in itself; each can only work if the lower strata work; each enables the higher strata; they are distinct; and yet are inseparable. They layer as six strata of ecosystems, or strata of distinct types of structures, interactions, and governance.

6 Inter-ecosystem the biggest scale, up to and including the global economy, the biosphere, etc.;

5 Inner-ecosystem everything around multiple organisations connected in some way into a network or ecosystem, such as the strongly connected ecosystem you replace your portfolio with;

4 Outer-organisational everything around stakeholders, capitals, etc. typically done via incorporation as a non-human person;

3 Inner-organisational everything around abstract roles, work processes, organisation design;

2 Inter-personal everything in the space between people, such as relationship structures and interactions, both explicit and implicit, culture, etc.

1 **Inner-personal** everything within and centred on each person, such as identity, inner voices and motivations, meaning-making, words, actions, thoughts, etc.

One way to see how each ecosystem emerges from the structures and interactions is that the structures tell the interactions how to flow, and the interactions give the structures their shape[2]. This interplay is the distinction I make between a system and an ecosystem.

That leads to governance. Think of governance as a way of choosing, or at least influencing, which path your ecosystem takes at each point the path could diverge. Governance spans predictable knowns; as well as known, unknown, and even unknowable unpredictables. Which means there is seldom one single right choice a priori, no matter how good your governance is, no matter how much information you have available.

Governance is as much art and intuition as it is deterministic science, and cannot always be clearly and unambiguously articulated.

Governance is in and between each of the six strata given on page 76. The better each individual governs themselves at stratum 1, the better we can govern all the way through to stratum 6, the global economy.

Because of the unpredictables, governance (in each stratum) will be at its best when you build structures and interactions making broad inclusion easy. Then you have the best chance, in every governance decision, of having someone in the room with that vital piece of experience, intuition, way of thinking, or being. At least include representatives of all who benefit and/or invest and/or bear some of the costs—the very quintessence of stakeholder theory.

Governance is a consequence of the structures and the interactions that deliver governance outcomes, and who is included in them.

Good governance begins with who has the right to engage in governance, with what balance of power versus other groups, and with what means to defend that right. This is why many contemporary approaches to improving governance fall short of expectations: they too narrowly focus proposals for modified governance on one aspect of the structure and/or the interactions. For example, no matter what values are developed in

---

[2] This is at the heart of General Relativity, which connects matter and space-time, and states that matter tells space-time how to curve, and space-time tells matter how to move.

those governing, if the structures exclude key stakeholders, or vital interactions are prevented, the outcomes will be inadequate. Even the best intentioned people can only take decisions from within their uniqueness: their paradigm, their meaning-making, their nature, and their awareness.

This is why building companies with stewards having significant governance power is important. The incorporation form used in the Evolutesix[6] ecosystem of companies has stewards, typically with between 26 and 51% of the governance power. Stewards need to be carefully chosen to represent all, especially those without a voice, and to bring in a sufficiently broad range of perspectives. Then they need to be constrained by the principles of stewardship to enable good governance and protect against poor governance. Mark Goyder's book *Entrusted: Stewardship For Responsible Wealth Creation*[51] gives good insights to this end. I also recommend that they are fairly remunerated, but have no share of dividends or capital gain, to remove incentives for self-interested actions.

Stewards, board members, executives, and other key people involved in governance need to be sufficiently mature (i.e., size of person) to fill the demands of their role (size of role). Specifically, each individual requires both sufficient meaning-making maturity and fluidity in the 28 post-logical forms of thought (in Chapters 8 and 9 of *Rebuild*[6]).

Once the foundation of *who* is adequate, then an appropriate, sufficiently powerful governance *process* can be chosen. The traditional voting process of today's shareholder meetings is inadequate for the governance required to execute an ergodic investment strategy. But fortunately we have developed very powerful methods that work well for a high diversity of conflicting perspectives and groups, like sociocratic consent, deep democracy, and the powerful blockchain-based approaches being developed in innovative DAOs (Decentralised Autonomous Organisations) etc.

An ergodic investment strategy is a stratum 5 strategy for ecosystems of companies with pooling and flows of one or more capitals between the companies at an ecosystem level. (If it is a single large multinational with multiple products in very different categories with divergent countercyclical responses to a given unpredictable, then your ergodic strategy is for an ecosystem spanning Strata 4 and 5.)

Contrast this with typical startup investment and business strategies today. These are all stratum 4 strategies, with no, or almost no stratum 5 elements. Even if you have a number of independent companies in your portfolio; even if the founders are part of a community of practice, and some level of collaboration is encouraged by the investors or the company leaders, it still falls far short of the systemic connectivity and interaction required to be an ergodic investment strategy.

Aligning business execution to the non-ergodic nature of business (including investing), is a disruptive innovation, a shift from anchoring in stratum 4 to anchoring in stratum 5.

This is as big as the geopolitical shift a few centuries ago in Europe from independent small principalities and cities to the Hanseatic league in central and northern Europe, and then to nation states. This progression at a geopolitical level, in a sense executing an ergodic social and economic strategy, has continued.

This resource pooling and interaction between fully or partially independent nations, states, or regions, I believe, is one of the underlying root causes of the successes of the EU, the US, China, India; and what might happen in Africa, Latin America, and other regions, as those countries collaborate more within and between regions.

Either investors, founders, and business leaders embrace this disruption and we all thrive, or we fail to embrace it and go the same way many wealthy families go: from rags to riches to rags in three generations.

You can only build a stratum 5 ergodic investment strategy by building single companies (stratum 4) with a multi-stakeholder incorporation, giving each stakeholder a fair share of governance and wealth. The bare minimum for a viable ergodic investment strategy is that all the companies pooling resources in the ecosystem have sufficient interlocking governance in each other, creating the key pillar of trust[3]. For example, a representative of the pool as a whole might have voting rights and board membership in each company.

Each individual company, and therefore the ecosystem as a whole, must include a sufficiently diverse range of representatives of all the capitals and stakeholders it touches. If key capitals or stakeholders are excluded, systemic trust is weakened, losing opportunities for collaboration and resource

---

[3] This in no way inherently reduces competition, so ought not lead to any anti-trust law issues. Recall, ergodic strategies break free of the competition—collaboration forced compromise. However, anti-trust laws will need updating to fully enable ergodic strategies.

pooling needed to approach the ergodic limit.

In stratum 4 governance we're only looking at the kind of governance that happens in shareholder meetings, such as decisions about board and executive roles, equity, debt, etc., not at the day-to-day governing of the work. That lies in stratum 3.

Yes, you can follow a limited ergodic investment strategy if the companies you bring together into an ecosystem are incorporated as a typical limited company, but it will be a fragile, sub-optimal execution.

Better, but still suboptimal, are ecosystems of cooperatives. They fare better than investor centric limited companies during financial downturns, because of the trust that cooperative governance gives. Staff are part of stratum 4 governance, so have the systemic trust needed to pool resources with the company by forgoing salary, by lending or investing their own money into the company, etc. Mondragon in 2008-2009 is an excellent example of an ecosystem of diverse cooperatives with resource pooling—see page 49.

The legal construct we use in our companies to build for an ergodic investment strategy is a multi-capital multi-stakeholder commons incorporation having an equitable distribution of governance and growth share across all capitals and stakeholders, called a FairShares Commons, and is optimised for ergodic strategies.

Think of a FairShares Commons more as a pattern language, not a specific concretisation; you can build it using one legal entity, or a combination of legal entities locked together. A FairShares Commons can be built on a limited company basis, on a cooperative basis, or as an association; it can be primarily for-profit or completely non-profit, or even 80% for-profit and 80% non-profit!

These can be constructed in most jurisdictions around the world, in some cases as single companies with multiple share classes, in other cases as a constellation of different company forms that together deliver the functionality.

FairShares Commons[6,52,53] and FairShares[52,54] organisations are well proven, having been built and run in a wide range of jurisdictions. These span the UK, Europe, the USA (the first USA FairShares, AnyShare, was incorporated in Delaware in 2016), and Canada. In England and Wales the coop version has already been approved as Model Articles by the FCA.

You can create a decentralised autonomous organisation as a FairShares Commons DAO, and perhaps wrap it with a mirror image incorporated entity, to get the best of both worlds. You can even build one on a spreadsheet for a one-month project.

In a FairShares Commons the shareholder meetings become stakeholder meetings that include all capitals and stakeholders. This sets the stage for building an antifragile stratum 5 fractional profit pooling ecosystem, because every company in your ecosystem that is a stakeholder in one specific company will take part in that company's stakeholder meeting[4].

The key characteristics every company ought to have in order to be strong enough to execute an ergodic investment strategy are listed below.

- The key capitals and stakeholders touched by the company's operations have appropriate voting and wealth rights.

- There is a distinct share class for each relevant capital and stakeholder type relevant to this business, with classes appropriate for suppliers, customers, and symbiotic partners (e.g., the city, research and education bodies, maybe the nation). This is especially important for the members of circles in a circular economy.

- General meetings, shareholder meetings, or whatever you call them are run in ways that fit your ergodic investment strategy. Instead of simple voting, use processes such as deep democracy, sociocratic consent voting, or Holacratic integrative decision-making.

- Powerful facilitation approaches (interactions) are used, such as those Adam Kahane[48] describes in his books, to best stay in the dynamic sweet spot of collaboration and competition with stakeholders that structurally cannot always agree with each other, and quite likely don't like nor trust each other.

- The different rights and obligations are treated distinctly in the construction of shares.

- Governance rights are weighted to best serve the sweet spot of your ergodic strategy. If one stakeholder group is numerically large and

---

[4]This is not about including all stakeholders in day-to-day operations, only the governance decisions that today require the investors to vote.

another numerically small, weight the vote such that the most enabling balance of power is established for your ergodic investment strategy. Neither the limited company, where the opinion with the most money wins, nor the cooperative, where the opinion with the most people wins, is good enough.

- All stakeholders have the same information rights.

- The company has stewards who are mandated to uphold the core principles of the company itself and the ecosystem as a whole. These typically centre on protecting and enabling the integrity of the company and ecosystem.

- The incorporation, to the best extent possible within the laws of the country, protects the freedom of this non-human legal person. At a minimum this means that the company cannot be removed from the ecosystem without full consent of the ecosystem, e.g., because it gets sold by the investors. (They can sell the financial value represented by investor shares.)

  The company can decide to partner with another equally free company, potentially a partnership tantamount to a merger. Equally, a company can decide to spin out 'children'.

  This is far more than simply preventing the company being sold; it is about having in place the structures and interactions fully enabling the company to act as a sovereign entity in its own right.

- The incorporation implements the key elements for the company to be a highly functioning commons of productive capacity across all the capitals it touches (input and output). This is the key enabler to ensure that each company is internally maximally net positive, and plays its fair share ensuring the entire ecosystem is maximally net positive.

- The company is designed to multiply all the capitals it touches, or at least to deliver its fair share of that multiplication within a larger ecosystem. It does not limit itself to growing financial capital at the cost of the other capitals. (Any business doing that is more an exchange mechanism converting natural and human capital to financial capital. It is not wealth creation, just as transferring money from your euro account into your dollar account is not generating wealth. In fact, transaction costs and losses erode wealth.)

- The generated wealth in each capital is partly retained in the company for future operations, and partly distributed to the investors of all capitals. For example, the staff who invest their human capitals get some fraction of both the profit (i.e., it doesn't all go to the financial investors as dividends) and the increase in the company's market cap.

- Build into your articles of incorporation or bylaws the right mixture of inventors, the company itself, the ecosystem of companies, through to the entire human population, having the right to use and/or change inventions. Or, as appropriate, being excluded from the right to use inventions. So that inventions, innovations, and other relevant aspects of the intellectual property are explicitly protected to best serve the interests of the larger ecosystem.

- Remuneration across all types of staff and other stakeholders contributing to company operations is optimised to maximise the benefit at an ecosystem level across all capitals and stakeholders. For example, a maximum remuneration ratio between the highest and lowest paid employee will usually lie between 3 and 20.

- The company's purpose is embedded in its incorporation as an explicit consequence of stating, in the incorporation, the external driver underlying the purpose. The company then has the freedom and capacity, as the external driver evolves over time, to update its purpose to match.

- Use more than one incorporated entity to get the functionality you need, if you cannot do it in your jurisdiction with a single incorporated entity. In some jurisdictions we've built a FairShares Commons using a combination of cooperatives, limited companies, and a trust, with each having an ordinary share in the operating company.

- Build your business engine for all the capitals your business touches, growing each of them, and maximising internal flows and pooling within and between each capital. Consider using an internal complementary currency system based on the blockchain or whatever other technology best suits.

- Use multi-capital accounting[21] to keep track of how effective your business engine is at growing each capital, and to maintain information transparency across all stakeholders to generate the trust you need.

- Structure the entire ecosystem according to these guidelines, perhaps as a holding company, incorporated in the same way as the individual companies in the ecosystem.

Note that these depend on the companies generating a surplus[5]. Which means each company must have an excellent product-market fit, enabling it to operate with sufficient profit.

And, as with nature's way of implementing capital pooling across all living species, profit pooling here actually increases each business's ability to generate surplus; and increases the positive impact of that surplus on all businesses, society, and nature.

Most likely you recognise some or all of the above elements. They all exist individually, or perhaps a few together, in forward-thinking organisations today. Each of these is part of a solution, but not a complete solution. This is often the way in disruptive innovation[55]. All too often, the innovation lies not in one magic ingredient; rather, it lies in the innovative confluence when all the ingredients are brought together. We will uncover even more elements of a solution once we build at scale. And it may always be *a* solution, never *the* solution.

Here are a few examples that I admire. Multi-stakeholder cooperatives address the weakness of mono-stakeholder cooperatives. Public Benefit Corporations (PBC) and the whole B-corp movement embed purpose and consider the benefit to multiple stakeholders in governance, but can lack the teeth and direct inclusion in governance and wealth sharing of all key stakeholders to truly live up to their potential. Equally, For Purpose, Steward Owned, and other approaches provide some of the foundations (e.g., prevent the company from being sold), but other key aspects needed for excellent execution of an ergodic investment strategy need to be added.

In the interests of brevity and staying focused on what this book is

---

[5]If you believe for-profit is the problem: an ergodic strategy requires profit, just as nature requires an oak tree to generate a massive surplus of acorns each year from the initial investment of a single acorn, to deliver antifragility.

about, namely the stratum 5 structures and interactions needed to execute an ergodic investment strategy, I'll not go deeper into the technical details of building a FairShares Commons here. If you want to start building, read Part 4 of Rebuild[6], which has 124 pages on building FairShares Commons companies.

In building a stratum 5 ecosystem of companies according to a maximising ergodic investment strategy, it's best if every company within this ecosystem is a sovereign entity satisfying the characteristics listed on page 81.

The key difference between what I point at with the word ecosystem, and what is often called a business ecosystem, is the presence of strong capital flows between companies and the use of at least one pooling mechanism. The pools will be one or more of those listed below; and, to have an ergodic investment strategy, at least one must be a financial pool spanning the entire ecosystem.

1. A fractional profit pool. At specific times every company puts an agreed percentage of their profit into the pool, and receives an agreed percentage of the pool in return.

2. A capital pool. At specific times every company puts an agreed percentage of their capital into the pool, and receives an agreed percentage of the pool in return.

3. Direct surplus profit distribution. A company's stakeholder companies receive a percentage of the quarterly or annual profit, akin to investor dividends. This can be pooled across all companies in the ecosystem, and the pool distributed.

4. Market cap growth distribution. A company's market cap growth is partly allocated to its stakeholder companies, akin to investor share price gains. This may be pooled first, which can be seen as an upgrade of the holding company structure we already know well.

5. Information pooling.

6. Staff time and skills pooling.

7. Intellectual capital pooling. IP, or certain types of IP, is pooled across all ecosystem members, e.g., a library of patents that everyone can use.

8. Manufactured capital pooling, e.g., a library of things that everyone can use.

9. Relationship and social capital pool.

Each of these pools requires the matching currency to facilitate the exchange, storage, and attribution of the capital. For financial pools you can use money, but also other currencies defined analogous to money, e.g. the Swiss WIR (CHW) (complementing the Franc), gold, or any other representation of financial capital, e.g., on the blockchain.

Time, skills, reputation, relationships are examples of capitals that cannot be pooled using money. Instead you need different currencies for each, such as a time currency (e.g., the Japanese Fureai Kippu), a reputation currency (a simple version is your ebay seller score), and currencies like the Terra[56] for natural resources. These enable economies of scale the larger the ecosystem becomes, and deliver maximum efficiency by eliminating the exchange losses that we currently have attempting to only use a financial currency for all kinds of capital.

These pools are governed by qualifying members in the entire ecosystem, including qualifying investors and each of the qualifying companies. Typically governance of the pools also includes representatives of each of the other key capitals and stakeholders in the ecosystem. Finally, because these pools are somewhat akin to a trust, governance includes stewards constrained by principles of stewardship.

You want to set this ecosystem-wide pool at the sweet spot across the range of competing objectives listed on page 52. If you transfer a very high percentage of profit or capital into the pool you get very close to perfect ergodicity, but increase the risk that you carry companies that ought to be closed down, and you risk reducing the drive towards innovation. On the other hand, if you go for a very small percentage, you run the risk that the very companies you need for a healthy, thriving ecosystem go prematurely bankrupt and are simply not there just when you need them.

From the limited data we have, for an ecosystem-wide pool of diverse and independent companies, 1% profit pooling may be enough to change the game, and 10% may be a healthy upper limit.

For pools that are not ecosystem wide, but only include companies that are very close to each other; or, if it is a small ecosystem in the sense of

Chapter 9, your sweet spot may well be higher. This is also where a capital pool, maybe even at 100% (recall Apple on page 47) may be best to optimise your ergodic investment strategy.

The pools in such a strongly connected ecosystem replicate many of the characteristics that make companies like Unilever or P&G an excellent investment. And they have, without compromise, many of the characteristics that make startups an excellent investment! So the best of both worlds, because pooling brings multiple diverse startups as close together as the brands in P&G are. When startups are very closely related (perhaps they are all key members of a single material circle in a circular economy) approaching a 100% pool may be the sweet spot.

After all, as you have seen (page 48), that is exactly what P&G is: 65 brands pooling their capital completely. An investment fund executing an equally powerful ergodic investment strategy would have 65 independent companies in a strongly connected ecosystem with a capital pool approaching 100%, and pools of all the other capitals, especially IP and staff.

You also want to optimise the size and nature of the pool. Is your context better served by a large single company pool, like P&G; a large multi-company pool with all the investment done by a single holding company; a diversified pool; a thematic pool; what kind of pool of pools might you have? All of these are choices, beyond the scope of this book, from which your unique ergodic strategy design emerges.

Optimising the diversity, size, and nature of the companies and the pool is especially relevant for companies that are part of a circular economy. If 10 companies form a single circle, an ergodic investment strategy optimises across the entire circle. This is the key element holding back transforming our economy to a net positive, regenerative, doughnut, circular etc. economy: we are trying to build a transformed economy using building blocks designed for pure competition. These are unable to deliver the trust and resource pooling essential for such an economy to have a chance of thriving.

Circular economies do best when companies early in the circle invest more heavily, so that companies later in the circle run at a lower cost. A circular economy investment strategy must optimise the performance across the entire circle. This requires a share of the profits and market capital growth of later companies in the circle go to earlier companies in the circle, and vice versa.

The first mover disadvantage that presents a significant barrier to starting circles is well addressed by an ergodic investment strategy.

Governance is the key here: the governance mechanisms need to deliver the systemic trust across the time taken for multiple cycles and across all companies and stakeholders for that to work.

To get to the right governance we need to go beyond the limitations imposed by our taking as an absolute unalterable fact other myths[6] in business, especially the myth that a company is something you can own, buy, or sell, like a car.

Instead, a company is a legal person, independent of the investors (who are also legal persons, either human or non-human). It is also a nexus of contracts. Investors are parties to contracts giving them a set of rights and obligations[57]. These rights and obligations are commonly bundled together into a limited number of à la carte options, and it is these contracts that can in some cases be sold.

The myth has become our conventional belief because the conventional bundles lead to the same outcomes as if investors owned the company, with the right to buy or sell it.

We can easily construct our own bespoke contracts, using existing company law, in almost all countries today. This opens up all the possibilities we need to build individual companies designed for an ergodic investment strategy.

In particular, we can have very different bundles for the financial, voting, and information rights. Early in my development of the FairShares Commons as a new way of building companies, I came across articles on hidden ownership and empty voting[58-63], the effects of this on individual businesses, and on the economy as a whole.

Empty voting is where an investor buys both voting shares and derivatives that pay out when the share price drops. If these derivatives pay out more than the shares are worth, then the investor has a financial incentive to vote against the interests of the company and cause it, or at least the share price, to collapse.

Hidden ownership is the reverse, where the investor sells the voting rights but retains ownership of the share's financial value.

In both cases, governance rights are split off from the financial rights. When I first read these papers it gave me a concrete example of the myth of investors owning[57,64] the company, and that with existing legislation we can do far more than most investors and entrepreneurs believe.

The work of Jordan Barry et al.[58] showed how empty voting and hidden ownership, coupled with information transparency, changes the entire stock market. They showed that including all key stakeholders in information rights increased individual company performance because it delivered a performance-optimising mix of the right kind of collaboration and the right kind of competition between stakeholders. Hitting this sweet spot is an element of an ergodic investment strategy. (Their work demonstrates the power of an ergodic strategy: the nature of capitalism can be changed with relatively small changes in structures and flows.)

So we now have the elementary formal structures and interactions we need to build individual companies, local ecosystems of these companies, and ultimately our global economy, to execute an ergodic strategy across all aspects of business.

Incorporate as a FairShares Commons, with this kind of inclusive spread of governance and information rights, and you have the foundation for governance of the ecosystem of all the companies you invest in. Many, if not all, of the companies will have a representative in the stakeholder meetings of other companies in your ecosystem. This means governance decisions can be taken that optimise at the level of the entire ecosystem—just what you need to execute your ergodic investment strategy.

This addresses one root cause of a typical investment fund underperforming versus potential: decisions maximise the returns from one startup, but leave even bigger returns lying on the table, and hence lower returns for the fund as a whole.

Let's turn now to how to build businesses capable of executing an ergodic investment strategy.

Once you've incorporated each company for an ergodic strategy, ideally using one of the FairShares Commons family of incorporations, and built the right ecosystem of such companies, the final step is to build an appropriate organisation: the ecosystem of work roles and tasks, and the two human ecosystems.

Within each company you need a standard self-governance method for human interactions for each individual to use for internal self-governance (stratum 1) and for governing the team (stratum 2). One approach, the Adaptive Way, I describe in Rebuild[6], and use daily in Evolutesix and with our clients. It integrates a wide range of complementary components that span everything from simply being able to recognise and articulate what you need through to today's most powerful evidence-based approaches to adult development.

There are many other effective ways of governing in strata 1 and 2. Find which one works for you and your company, and then use it.

Then there's the question of the work itself: defining roles, filling them, what work is done, and how it's done. This is stratum 3. We typically use sociocracy or Holacracy. There are many other approaches to building fluid organisations—I strongly recommend building what works for you by looking at what has worked for others, and then optimising for your specific context and ergodic investment strategy.

It's important that everyone in the ecosystem is using the same approach in strata 1 to 3, to maximise efficiencies. Then, when someone moves from one company to another in your strongly connected ecosystem, they will be able to interact effectively and efficiently with their new colleagues—and get up to full productivity fast.

A few closing thoughts about how to design and optimise your unique ergodic investment strategy, which we will expand on in our next book.

Look at nature for ideas. Nature thrives because it pools all capitals at all scales, from within a single celled amoeba, through entire ecosystems like the African Savannah, to the entire planet. All of these at all scales are cross-linked, pools of pools, etc.

These pools only exist when they are running, not when they are static. So optimise the pool as a running ecosystem, for those times when the flows and interactions are extreme, and when they are near the average. Think of an entire catchment area of a river: does it run optimally as a nearly dry river bed in a drought, as a raging flood spreading for kilometres on either side of the banks, or as a steady river?

This also requires your pooling mechanism itself to be dynamic and responsive to the changing context. Your profit fraction ρ going into the pool may be quite low when the whole economy is booming, and may be quite high when everyone is struggling. The governance itself needs to be robust enough to work across all contexts, and the governance structures and interactions themselves must be able to change. This also means that governance must be independent of any single strong person, but rather has well-trained transformational facilitators[48] well versed in even getting people who neither agree nor trust each other to collaborate for both their individual benefit and the overall benefit.

In fact, your entire ergodic strategy is itself an adaptive strategy[6], one that changes as fast as the change drivers in the external environment. Excellent execution of an ergodic strategy demands even more adaptive capacity of the leaders and the organisation[6].

Maximising organisational adaptive capacity is why you must incorporate with powerful approaches, like the FairShares Commons, and not with a standard C-corp, plc, etc., because you are incorporating for knowable and unknowable unpredictables as part of a strongly connected profit pooling ecosystem of other companies.

To succeed in business always requires alignment with the laws of nature, including its inherent non-ergodic capital change processes. This alignment is only possible if the company has the freedom to move as far and fast as its driver moves. Especially, it must be free of the outright control of any single person or narrow stakeholder group. Otherwise it is all too likely to underperform, because it falls back to a "knowable knowns" strategy.

If we only build and strategize for what we know and can predict, then we will have far too little flexibility to keep our balance when unknowable unpredictables come our way. And so the business will collapse and the investors will lose their money. History is littered with examples: from Nokia and Kodak in the more recent past, through the companies that once shipped ice from cold climes to the wealthy in warm climes, and back to businesses lost in the mists of time.

To execute your ergodic investment strategy, you need to build systems and interactions that have the right blend of the relevant factors in the right quantities. Your unique strategy may not need all the systems and interactions mentioned in this book; and it may have others. I hope it does have others that I've not even thought of, as this is a blue ocean[66] space ready for innovation!

---

[6]Norman Wolfe's *The Living Organisation*[65] framework eases designing and delivering an adaptive strategy, and this book shows why such an approach outperforms.

CHAPTER 9

Why Bigger *is* Better

*Net positive companies adopt a mindset that the company
doesn't actually belong to them, but to all stakeholders.*
—Polman and Winston in Net Positive[9]

Let's get even more practical ideas from nature's execution of ergodic strategies to create thriving, antifragile life. But, to see clearly in order to then apply what you learn from nature, it's vital to avoid two common misunderstandings of how evolution works.

Firstly, most people misunderstand the word 'fittest' (in the phrase 'survival of the fittest') to mean the same as 'strongest'. In Darwin's time the word commonly meant how well something fits into the space it's in. As in, "you'll never fit that car into that gap" followed by the sounds of breaking glass and crunching metal along with "I told you so".

So the phrase 'survival of the fittest' means that those species survive that fit better into the space in their environment. By using (as is typical in business and economics) the inappropriate frame of reference of strength, rather than the appropriate frame of reference of fitting a certain niche, we end up with businesses that are somewhat like a bull in a china shop: very strong, but such a poor fit to the context that much of value is damaged.

We are now dealing with the consequences of centuries of building ever stronger bulls in ever weaker china shops. Even worse, we're not seeing it because much in business and economics is a cargo cult, not evidence based.

The second error is the belief that natural selection is about single animals. Instead, compelling research over the past few decades, described in Wilson's book[47], shows more and more clearly that evolution acts at the group level and even at the level of the entire ecosystem.

One experiment compared:

1. Individual selection: let the strongest two rabbits breed; then repeat the process a number of times, letting only the strongest individuals breed.

2. Group selection: work at the group level, choose the best two groups of rabbits, let them breed, and repeat.

Comparing these two alternatives, the end result is that the strongest rabbit from individual selection is equivalent to the average, or even the weakest rabbit in group selection.

This only seems mysterious when you falsely assume that nature's dynamics are ergodic. Only if that were true would rabbits evolve individually towards the ensemble average. But nature is not ergodic, so rabbits evolve individually towards the path-dependent time expectation value, which is smaller.

Nature knows this. The blend of collaboration and competition we see in nature *is* the ergodic maximising strategy to optimise nature's natural capital investment, given life's multiplicative and non-ergodic processes.

Whether you are talking about the growth of algae on a pond, doubling every day; or rabbits; or wolves; each of them grows over some natural time period as a percentage of the starting value. In other words, the dynamics are multiplicative and non-ergodic; so you must use the matching non-ergodic multiplicative statistical equations to get the right answer.

Then it becomes perfectly clear that some level of resource pooling is the best strategy for individual success; and through that for the group as a whole. The dynamics of biomass capital growth mathematically ties individual success to having a group pooling resources, and so you naturally get evolution acting at the group level, i.e., the level of the resource pool as a whole. The fittest individuals are those that build the most effective resource pooling groups.

Keep firmly in mind: collaboration within groups of animals and plants automatically comes out of the mathematics[41,42], without necessarily requiring behavioural, values, or other explanation. These may also be part of the complete set of reasons why, but are not the root cause.

The right level of competition and collaboration emerges naturally in nature. Neither competition nor collaboration alone is 'right'; rather it's the context-dependent balance that nature harnesses.

I use the word group, because we are not only talking about homogeneous groups of the same species[47]; we're also talking about heterogeneous groups of different species. Up to and including collaborating with the enemy[7]. An entire natural ecosystem could be seen as a resource pooling economy, where even predator and prey are structured by nature into both competing and collaborating in a way that leads to resource pooling.

Ergodicity, and the benefits of an ergodic investment strategy, are also seen very clearly when comparing societies[41]. Sometimes a higher level of individualism and competition makes best use of unpredictables; and in other contexts, a higher level of collaboration and resource pooling makes best use of unpredictables. Purely one or purely the other is not always healthy in the short term, and certainly not for the long term.

So wherever you look there's more than enough evidence that the most intelligent investment strategy is an ergodic one that has an optimum blend of collaboration (resource pooling between multiple entities across all capitals) and competition (resource accumulation within an entity across all capitals). These entities might be single natural legal persons, groups of natural persons, single non-human legal persons, or groups of non-human legal persons.

This optimum blend is what we need in businesses for business to meet all needs.

With this blend, following the true multiplicative, non-ergodic nature of business, it becomes clear that being net positive across all capitals (including profit in financial capital) is the most intelligent strategy for all stakeholders. Whatever your investment objective, you are best served with such an ergodic investment strategy. Even if you are only interested in financial returns.

If you have a pension fund's long-term horizon, or that of a family office etc., you will be better served with an ergodic investment strategy delivering a strongly connected, resource pooling ecosystem of highly diverse companies.

If you are investing with an impact or venture philanthropy objective, expecting growth in human and / or environmental as well as financial capital, you want an ergodic strategy, optimised for all the capitals touched.

If you are investing with a net positive, regenerative, circular economy, multi-solving objective then nothing other than an ergodic strategy can deliver.

Even if you are investing simply for emotional objectives and the thrills of winning and losing, build your investment strategy fully informed by the fact that individual business processes are non-ergodic. Choose where to place your bets in full awareness of both the fact that unpredictables dominate and that they multiply, not add. So your skill, the patterns that you see, are far from reliable indicators of what's going to happen in the future.

Scale increases antifragility and increases the individual benefits when you execute an ergodic strategy. Let's look again at nature for an example of a superb ergodic investment strategy at scale. Natural ecosystems are at their most antifragile when they have huge numbers of living entities in them, distributed over the widest diversity of types of life, from the smallest virus through to the largest plants, fungi, and animals. There is an optimum level of connectivity, or flow of capitals across the entire ecosystem, and huge shared resource pools, like groundwater, the oceans, the air, and many more.

This is the difference between a system and an ecosystem, and why much of what we call an ecosystem in business falls short. In an ecosystem, both the structures and the interactions or flows are optimised. Then much happens with effortless action because it is emergent from the fundamental essence of each element interacting with the others, each according to its true nature.

Nature governs these pools as a commons. Not via top-down control, instead governance emerges from the positive complicity between all elements of nature being at the stable point of a maximised ergodic strategy.

The antifragile elements enabling life on earth to thrive, despite, or even because of, the non-ergodic growth dynamics of nature's processes, only emerge once the ecosystem is sufficiently strongly connected and large. For some, only once it's as large as a planet.

You see other examples of capital pools governed as a commons throughout human history. Elinor Ostrom's research[6,67] showed how highly functioning commons have historically been governed, and the recent book of Michel Bauwens, *Peer to Peer: The Commons Manifesto*[20] gives many recent examples of highly functioning commons. Open source software is intellectual capital pooling, an ergodic strategy in action, and why it punches way above its weight.

In essence, a highly functioning commons is one way of executing an ergodic strategy, taking non-ergodic dynamics closer to the ergodic maximum.

To execute a non-ergodic investment strategy well, we're going to need to have all scales. Sometimes bigger is better. We need strongly connected ecosystems from the scale of the planet through the scale of the economy of a small village all the way down to each of our personal economies.

At each scale, sufficient antifragility becomes effortless, a simple emergent consequence of executing an optimal ergodic strategy at that scale. Failing to execute an ergodic strategy, as in business today, requires a constant external inflow of capital(s), as covered in Chapter 4.

A classic example is the amount of financial and natural capital we consume in the way we are running our economy, leading to a footprint 2.5× the earth. Were we running on an ergodic strategy across the global economy, we would all have a good life without needing one and a half additional earths.

Businesses today, blind to the non-ergodic nature of business, underperform, which drives excessive and needless resource consumption.

Luck at scale is a vital, but under-recognised, component of the real strategy behind large funds.

Compare exiting within 10 years, a core element of a typical VC fund strategy, with the buy and hold strategy, Warren Buffett's value investing approach. His investments are in large companies, and some have a sufficiently wide range of geographic markets and product categories that the company itself has a kind of internal capital pool, and its strategy is a small step towards the ergodic limit.

Few VC funds have any of this, and instead depend far more than they realise on luck. Hence the importance to a VC of unicorns and timing the exit: hitting the peak created by unpredictables and the inherent non-ergodic nature of business. VCs need that one big unicorn exit for the fund to return what was promised to the limited partners, because their investment strategies are blind to non-ergodic dynamics.

The same applies in many of today's funds. The strategies driving fund size and a unicorn focus are an aftermarket patch to correct for business plans and investment strategies being blind to the non-ergodic nature of business. Except, of course, when the fund is executing an ergodic strategy: then it might be large and have many diverse unicorns as a consequence of being a large and diverse fractional profit pooling ecosystem.

The current trend of ever larger funds is a consequence of strategies that only work as intended if the business could grow capital ergodically. Or if you rely on luck. The larger the fund, the more likely you are to strike it lucky and have a unicorn. Then you need to exit before the luck runs out.

This is simply an artefact of the non-ergodic nature of business today. Look again at Figure 3.5. You see very clearly that, across 50 equally likely projections of the business you are about to invest in, some of them do quite well, at least if you exit somewhere between years 5 and 10. Other projections go bankrupt within the first two years. Remember, these are simply projections of one single business, using the correct statistics for non-ergodic, multiplicative capital dynamics.

While the capital of many projections increases at first, all of them decrease eventually, and so your expected outcome is bankruptcy. Projections that yield a positive return, *if* you exit at the right time during your 10 year fund, yield a positive return because of luck—a beneficial sequence of unknowns.

So part of the reason why timing and the number of startups you invest in appears to be the key strategic differentiator between successful and unsuccessful investors is because of the incorrect use of ergodic statistics in a non-ergodic business world.

Another kind of patch is the small funds that specialise in one specific sector (say, fintech). This is commonly labelled 'investing in the fintech ecosystem'. A few of them will be more lucky than average, and a few will be less lucky than average. But they all under-perform versus the ergodic limit because each business implicitly assumes ergodicity, and it's seldom a sufficiently strongly connected ecosystem.

However, were they to use an ergodic strategy between the companies, they would likely take a step closer to the ergodic limit. Link enough of these together into a truly diverse (i.e., not just fintech) and a large enough ecosystem and you can get to the ergodic upper limit.

Bigger is better, because you:

- have more businesses, increasing the flow of capitals across your ecosystem (as you saw in Chapter 8) and creating bigger pools; and

- have a larger range of business types with different exposures to different known, unknown, and unknowable unpredictables.

Bigger is also better because much of what is pivotal for each business's success along the path is an unknowable unpredictable. Think of Nokia, beginning with paper, adding electricity generation, pivoting to rubber when near bankruptcy and being acquired by a rubber company, finally pivoting purely to telecommunications, and then collapsing because it was unable to pivot from vanilla cell phones to smartphones.

The bigger the ecosystem, especially the more strongly connected it is, the greater the probability that it, as a whole, has the curiosity and capacity to support curious exploration, leading to effortless pivoting within it and across it. Far lower cost and higher probability of success than Nokia's history, where each shift was quite effortful because the scale was just not there.

Ergodic strategies also address the very valid objection against large companies becoming monopolies, but without losing the benefits of scale vital to certain services. For example, modern platforms like Google and Facebook must be big to do the job. A strongly connected resource pooling ecosystem of independent companies is simultaneously big and small: the ecosystem collaborates enough to do the whole job of Google, but each individual company is small and can change fast, driven by competition. Wikipedia has elements of this, in the very wide pool of independent contributors.

Part of what makes a bigger ecosystem better is that it has more diversity, yielding a wider range of complementary businesses that have countercyclical responses to a given unpredictable. Imagine if Zoom and Get Your Guide had been in one ecosystem.

You know you're getting to a viable ecosystem size when you start to have tension between companies. This is what you're looking for. You need the diversity and scale that leads to arguments, even to disagreements that persist.

And the same is true in each company—if there's not enough arguing, if only one opinion is dominant independent of validity, it's either not diverse enough, or people and systems are not yet ready to fully enable an internal ergodic strategy.

So the bigger your ecosystem becomes, the more leverage you have to execute a powerful and nuanced ergodic investment strategy.

Recall the suppliers to P&G in China on page 50 operating an informal unstructured pool of various human capitals. Time, experience, and skills were to some extent pooled. When this becomes embedded in formal structures and interactions, and governed well, this would be equivalent to a small, perhaps 0.1% human capital pool.

Startup studios and accelerators also do a basic form of human capital pooling by providing fractional staff, such as fractional chief finance and marketing officers, and by running regular community of practice sessions for founders and other staff members to learn from each other's experiences.

Let's look at two concrete examples of approaches that currently require effort, pushing against the system to make them happen, but that naturally emerge when an ergodic investment strategy reaches a large enough scale: Polman and Winston's *Net Positive*[9], and John Fullerton's regenerative programme[11,13,68].

Let's start with *Net Positive*. Polman and Winston lay out the following five principles.

1. Ownership of all impacts and consequences, intended or not.

2. Operating for the long-term benefit of business and society.

3. Creating positive returns for all stakeholders.

4. Driving shareholder value as a result, not a goal.

5. Partnering to drive systemic change.

These are best achieved by, and emerge as a natural consequence of, executing an ergodic strategy well and at scale: the inherent unpredictability of events and non-ergodic nature of capital dynamics leads to capital pooling, which is best when including all capitals and stakeholders, including future generations, in wealth share and governance.

Equally, once you look at success as stratum 5, the success of the whole fractional profit pooling ecosystem, all five will be present because you no longer see a division between 'us' and 'them', 'today' and 'tomorrow'.

You can go the other way. Start with these five as overarching design requirements, act in accordance with the non-ergodic nature of all capitals, and you will have an ergodic investment strategy.

John Fullerton's eight principles of a regenerative economy[11], listed below, can also be seen as either guiding principles for, or emerging as top-level outcomes of, successfully executing an ergodic investment strategy. As with the five principles of net positive, once you add, as an overarching given, the non-ergodic nature of business processes, you get an ergodic investment strategy, and vice-versa.

1. In right relationship.

2. Views wealth holistically.

3. Innovative, adaptive, responsive.

4. Empowered participation.

5. Honors community and place.

6. Edge effect abundance.

7. Robust circulatory flow.

8. Seeks balance.

In a large enough ecosystem of companies built to execute an ergodic investment strategy as close as possible to the ergodic limit for financial capital, all eight principles are naturally present because they each take you closer to the ergodic limit and make the ecosystem more antifragile. Conversely, each is a powerful guiding principle for building such an ecosystem: without them, you'll be under-performing versus the ergodic limit.

This is equally true for the *Net Zero Business Models*[69] of Montgomery and Van Clieaf. Ergodic strategies are powerful enablers for their net zero business models.

There is also a mutually beneficial relationship between ergodic investment strategies and integral investing, as described in Mariana Bozesan's[70] and Robert Dellner's[71] books. They cover how integral investing can be seen as the next stage of investing, delivering the outcomes of impact investing, philanthropy and standard return driven investing, enabled by individuals' inner values progressing from ego-centric to world-centric.

World-centric values lead to the kind of business behaviours that ergodic strategies lead to. If we replace business plans invalidly assuming ergodic capital dynamics with plans using valid non-ergodic dynamics, an ego-centric self-interested homo economicus pools capitals because pooling is in their self interest; and the world-centric person pools capitals because it is also good for the world.

Also consider Eve Poole's seven toxic assumptions[72] in capitalism. Of these, three arise because of the original toxic and false assumption that capital growth processes are ergodic. When you use the correct non-ergodic formulation of this book, you will see that these assumptions are false. They become the three below.

1. Pure competition is a strategy for economic failure and lacks fiduciary responsibility in a non-ergodic world. Instead, collaboration and competition is the optimal individual strategy.

2. The invisible hand becomes visible, and is quite different to economists' usual concept. It is merely an ergodic strategy, explicit or emergent, nudging towards the ergodic limit in a non-ergodic world.

3. Utility theory itself becomes visible as, in part, an after-market patch economics invented to correct for the errors[42] caused by falsely assuming ergodicity. This is a patch that is no longer needed, especially given the relativity of each of our perceptions of value[6].

Poole's remaining four assumptions are addressed when building businesses as FairShares Commons, incorporated including all capitals, without investor primacy.

Bookstaber's *The End of Theory*[73], gives a more academic understanding of why economics falls short in crises and times of rapid change. Ergodic strategies address the four root causes he describes: computational irreducibility, emergent phenomena, non-ergodic dynamics, and radical uncertainty.

Ergodic thinking also shines a light on why and how other approaches work, and how they can be optimised. For example, impact investing, venture philanthropy, and all the other valid frameworks, including those in the footnote[1], and many more not mentioned here.

---

[1] *Triple Bottom Line*, many aspects of the blueprints for regenerating R3.0 and the whole

What really matters for Polman and Winston's *Net Positive*[9], John Fullerton's programme, and all the rest, is that, when following an ergodic strategy, their principles are all naturally done. And they are naturally done with effortless action, because there's no compromise between these principles and approaching the ergodic limit for financial wealth growth. These principles emerge from, and in some cases flesh out, the execution of an excellent ergodic investment strategy, and so serve as superb boxes on a checklist to measure how close your strategy and execution is capable of getting you to the ergodic limit. Ergodic finance and ergodicity economics shines a light on the essence of our world.

An ergodic strategy also opens up better ways of executing the default strategies of Chapter 4. For example, the staff and investors in a FairShares Commons company have aligned long-term interests, so the staff are very likely to agree to a reduction in remuneration during economic downturns, knowing that they will benefit later from their share of surplus profit and capital gain if the company survives. They have trust in this because they have governance power.

An ergodic strategy also has no need for the 'equilibrium economy' assumed in much of economics; in fact, the further you are from equilibrium, the bigger the benefit of an ergodic investment strategy. So for anyone investing for the transition into the next economy—whether you focus on climate change, resource depletion, AI as the driver of that transition—your best chance is an appropriate ergodic investment strategy.

It's time to start a new discipline in finance, matching the emerging ergodicity economics: ergodic finance. It's finance that works in the actual world, regardless of any ideology, because it works with the actual dynamics of capital.

---

regenerative movement, circular economy, Prosocial[74], the entire emerging peer to peer economy[20], Doughnut Economics[75], impact investing, Zebras Unite, multi-capital accounting of Mark McElroy, Steward-Owned for purpose businesses (e.g. the Purpose Foundation), sociocracy, Holacracy, Deliberately Developmental Organisations of Kegan[37], Future Capital's work, Rethinking Economics, *Rethinking Organizations*[76] of Laloux, and Norman Wolfe's *the Living Organisation*[65]

CHAPTER 10

Your Life

Life is just one damned thing after another.

—*anon*[77]

Unpredictables are the essence of life, and you've now read about powerful ways of benefitting from unpredictables in business. Harness them, instead of trying to make everything predictable.

You can also benefit from unpredictables in your life, by following a life strategy based on the true non-ergodic nature of life. Then you'll see unpredictables, both beneficial and detrimental, as invitations to unscripted potential benefit.

Everything you've read up until now is as relevant to you (a human person) as it is to every incorporated entity (a non-human person) you invest one or more capitals in. This chapter shows what an ergodic investment strategy means across all the non-financial capitals.

We humans have been following ergodic investment strategies with our human, natural, and manufactured capitals ever since we emerged on the planet.

The capital dynamics and the equations described in this book hold as true for your self-esteem, your reputation, your knowledge, and for many other aspects of our lives, as they do for your financial capital growth, and in nature for the biomass of a virus spreading around the planet, for a forest, or the total mammalian biomass on earth.

I (Jack) have had some superb times in my life, and some very dark times. At times I've evaluated my life in the moment as wanting. At times I've doubted that my life has purpose.

Looking back over my life, just like in the commencement address of Steve Jobs referred to on page 110, I can only join the dots backwards. One of the random unpredictables was meeting Graham in London in 2015 when I spoke at the Rethinking Economics conference, and was asked a question by him about the impact of the developmental maturity of thought leaders on the state of economics. (You can see the answer that Graham and I came up with in *Rebuild*.)

Because of this, I've long realised that my life is a path, and so cannot be evaluated in the moment. As in many traditions, the only point where I can evaluate my life is right at the end, as I look back along the entire path. Or maybe even only after seven or more generations! And even then any evaluation of my life is flawed, because too much is an unknowable unknown.

I've known that my path has been what it is because of key unpredictables, beginning with the genes that I was born with, and the time and context I grew up in.

Consider Graham and myself (Jack): each of our natural talents, and life paths to date, integrated with the unpredictables, led to both *Rebuild* and this book. Talent and unpredictables go together. Inseparably.

I (Graham) recall clearly in 2013 suddenly realising that I am my life path, not just that part of me that I'm conscious of now. And, unlike in the world of physical companies, my imagination enables me to pool alternate life paths in parallel universes. When I'm feeling angry, I can imagine the feeling of contentment in a different universe, and pool that feeling with my anger to move towards a functional, integrated balance.

I grew up in South Africa, where the philosophy of Ubuntu (see the glossary) has played a seminal role in the country's responses to unpredictables, and hence the path it is going down.

An excellent example was the creation of the Truth and Reconciliation Committee. These experiences have made it clear to me that I am who I am because everyone I've directly or indirectly interacted with is who they are. And vice versa.

I came to these insights, began building our ergodic ecosystem venture studio Evolutesix, and wrote this book because my career as a physicist trained me in the application of path integrals to non-ergodic processes in fundamental particle physics. I've long used this lens, taking different business decisions to my colleagues, even when I wasn't able to explain why.

My life is a path of unpredictables, and I can only connect the dots looking back.

I may not know what good my life is now, and perhaps I never will; but as Lawrence Ford often says and writes[78], *'you're here for a reason'*. You just may not have lived long enough to see the reason in full.

We humans know intuitively that we only have one life path to live, that along that path various events happen, and these events multiply each other.

All it takes is one massive windfall and your whole life, and the lives of your children and grandchildren, benefit. Equally, all it takes is one massive setback, and your whole life, and that of your children and grandchildren, can be derailed.

Especially if that massive setback means you never have children in the first place. Or if that massive setback means you are born into some systemically disadvantaged group, or are enslaved.

Because we intuitively grasp ergodic investment strategies applied to ourselves, we form communities, tribes, nations, professional membership bodies—and companies.

What's happening in each of these communities is that an ergodic investment strategy for one or more of the six capitals is being implemented.

Early in human history, it was primarily about pooling the natural, intellectual, social, relationship, and time capitals we needed to live. If one person managed to hunt down a buck and brought that home to the tribe, the whole tribe had meat. If another found mushrooms, the whole tribe ate them. And if a third brought back water and fruit, the whole tribe had everything it needed.

Each of us once knew intuitively that whether we came home at the end of the day with food or not was out of our control; an unpredictable. Some attributed it to the gods, and developed all kinds of rituals to try turning the unpredictable into a predictable. And whether these worked or not, we saw patterns and believed that they worked, often creating cargo cults, and sometimes by accident or decent empirical testing creating something that truly did work.

Looking through the lens of an ergodic investment strategy, we can now see that behind what has worked throughout human history are ergodic strategies: when enough people pooled the capitals they needed, then the probability that all had enough resources to thrive individually and collectively was significantly greater.

By coming together into a community and pooling resources we are acting from strongly self-interested motives to maximise our own individual long-term benefit in a non-ergodic world. A community is a capital pooling and governance mechanism; the core are the different kinds of human, social, and relationship capitals; often natural and manufactured capital too.

Pooling in a community only seems to require altruism and various other explanations if we imagine the world to be ergodic. Actually it's simply a mathematical strategy optimising our own life path to be as close to the ergodic limit as possible.

Of course empathy, altruism, and all the other values, emotions, and behaviours play a role. But the more we understand what strategies are fit for purpose in our non-ergodic world the more we see that empathy, altruism, etc., can easily be explained, at least in part, as an ergodic investment strategy[41,44] for nature to maximise its return on investment of its life's capital.

It explains why belonging is so important, and why we still form into tribes. Today's tribes are no longer solely based on the family and geography of your birth, but also on multiple other criteria that discriminate between 'in the tribe' and 'outside the tribe'. Some criteria are quite informal, others are very formal, like being an accredited lawyer licensed to practice.

That the needs to belong, to maintain respect, to be seen and accepted, are universally of high priority reflects our intuitive ergodic life strategy. This is why Job 2 (the effort put into protecting oneself) can, in many companies, take well over half of every employee's effort, leaving less than half available for the job that they were hired to do, Job 1. (See the glossary and *Rebuild*.)

Losing your membership of the tribe was originally a near certainty that you would soon run out of food and die. Even today, in some professions, losing your reputation, especially losing your membership of the professional body, makes it a near certainty that you will be ostracised and cease earning money. At least until you have managed to reinvent yourself and your self-identity. Which is why major innovation in such professions usually comes from outsiders.

And so we go to great lengths to avoid being ostracised, or anything reducing our belonging to our group. We construct our identity, our beliefs and values, according to the norms of the group or groups that we need to belong to. This is what makes it so hard to change our beliefs and practices, even in the face of clear evidence that we should do so; it requires us to change our identity, akin to allowing some part of our self to die; but more, it places us at risk of being ostracised from the group—so triggering an existential threat response[6,24].

How often do you see individuals taking detrimental decisions? Detrimental now, and even more so in the future, to them, their children, and their grandchildren? This is why so few businesses, so few individuals, recognise, in time, a big disruption coming at speed, failing to take even the last possible chance to let go of every old 'truth', even though that 'truth' is now going to take everyone down.

It's why people continued to invest their capitals (financial, and also human, intellectual, and social) into Kodak's chemical photographic products long after digital had begun accelerating. This, despite the fact that Kodak invented digital photography! Membership of the Kodak tribe required belief in chemical products, even though more and more individuals in Kodak could see that the emerging digital disruptive innovation was coming.

It's like staying in the area where you were born even though the river that you depend on for life was rearranged a month ago by a flood, which moved it 30 km west, and now it's drying up. Our economy is at that point now; except that we are blocking the source of the river we depend on, and we've yet to put in the scale of effort needed to bring the river back to the strength human life depends on.

Our biology[24] is a key barrier to seeing, clearly and timely, new kinds of threats and then acting effectively and fast. Multiple parts of the brain are networked together into what is called the default mode network, which kicks into action whenever we face an existential threat. Importantly, it cannot distinguish between threats to your physical or psychological self. And the other challenge today is that it can only work off the old patterns that it learnt dealing with old threats. It fails us badly when a new threat requires us to act in ways that would cause harm in the old context.

In a completely new context, for example when disruptive innovation has begun, our brain tries to merely assimilate the new context into the old to continue doing what is always done. Only once the felt tension caused by the cognitive dissonance gets bigger than the affective tipping point does the drive to change get big enough and clear enough to accept the existential risks of trying out new response patterns. Which can mean leaving everything that has enabled them up to now, such as their cherished home and tribe.

For innovators, the affective tipping point is quite low, and so they leave their old tribe and build a new one at the first sign of a disruptive innovation[55]. For early adopters, they leave the old tribe and join the new as first followers soon after it's founded. And so it continues, until the laggards realise that they're the last ones left in a tribe long past its expiry date. *How Minds Change*[24] by David McRaney is an excellent book on this whole theme, although it would be even better with an explicit understanding of the non-ergodic dynamics underpinning collective resistance to change.

£7,000 a year—that's the hit to your salary if you come from a working-class family is the title of a recent report[79] by Alan Milburn, the chair of the Social Mobility Foundation. You will likely now recognise that this report describes the symptoms of path-dependent differences.

Milburn's report showed that, if you are a white male from a working class background the gap is not quite as big on average, only £6,718 a year less than people from better off backgrounds doing the same job as you.

The gap gets bigger when you move into professional roles, and the higher the pay scale: more than £8,000 for CEOs, finance managers, management consultants and solicitors.

Now this is exactly what you expect for wealth growth when you're dealing with path-dependent non-ergodic wealth growth dynamics. The path you are on today began on the path your parents were on, which itself began on the path their parents were on, going back generations. The seven generations timespan used in many ancient traditions is a good proxy for how long unpredictables can affect a life.

The other numbers make this even more clear: if you're a woman, you're paid on average £9,450 less than a man doing the same work. Or, if your life path is a fork of life paths that began in, say, Bangladesh or the Caribbean, you will be earning £10,432 and £8,770 less respectively than your white peers in the same jobs.

This data again underpins the importance of where your life path starts, which is a consequence of your parents' and grandparents' life paths. And this book shows how resource pooling of any or all of the six capitals across a sufficiently large and diverse group of individuals takes them all, individually and collectively, closer to the ergodic maximum in financial capital. This has power that we are simply not tapping into to close systemic gaps, benefitting individuals and society as a whole. And it's about pure maths, not ideology.

Everything you've seen so far in this book is not just for companies; it all has a real impact on your personal financial wealth, and your wealth in self esteem, relationships, knowledge capital, health, personal and positional power, and much more.

The change dynamics of all of these capitals, including your personal wealth, mostly follow the same multiplicative dynamics described in this book, are path-dependent, and are changed beneficially or detrimentally by the unpredictables that have happened, and will happen, along your path.

These capitals also have multiplicative impacts on each other. A beneficial unpredictable will increase your financial wealth more if you are simultaneously wealthy in power, self esteem, intellectual capital, etc. Equally, a detrimental unpredictable may have less effect on you if you are wealthy in all of these other capitals; except if this detrimental unpredictable triggers you being ostracised from belonging to the groups from which you derive social, relationship, and power capitals. (See the movie *Trading Places*.)

I class the genes you were born with and the heritage you were born into as part of the unpredictables. After all, unless your beliefs include things like karma, these were not choices you made, but just the toss of the dice.

Steve Jobs' life illustrates the impact of pooling to achieve individual success. He advanced the computing industry by 10 years, according to Bill Gates, when he brought proportional fonts to the Apple screen. This was one step in a connected path dominated by unpredictables, as Jobs said in his 2005 commencement address at Stanford[80]. In it he described how he'd realised he could only connect the dots that made him successful looking backwards. He said that part of the sequence of unpredictables that led to him introducing proportional fonts was him dropping into a calligraphy class at university.

The sequence of unpredictables goes further back. He dropped out of university when he realised that his university fees were being paid for out of the retirement savings of his adoptive parents. He then started simply dropping into his own personal curriculum of classes, following his curiosity and intuition to learn what he wanted to learn, as he had no idea what he wanted to do with his life, nor any idea which university classes might help him. Nor did he want the degree itself, just the knowledge and skills.

Jobs was able to do this because: he had friends who were resource pooling with him (a floor or sofa to sleep on, relationships, time); the Hare Krishna temple was resource pooling food with him once a week; and because Reed College was resource pooling intellectual capital with him.

As talented and competitive as Steve Jobs was, the huge growth of his personal and business financial capital could only be created because of this resource pooling, enabling him to harness unpredictables when they emerged.

Jobs certainly intuitively realised, even if he couldn't put it into these words, that our lives are non-ergodic paths dominated by unpredictables, and the sequence of one damn thing after another can only be joined up by looking backwards, not predicted and controlled looking forwards.

He probably also realised, at some level, that resource pooling was a competitive edge in his personal life and in Apple's business success. For example, in Chapter 6 I describe how his biggest innovation was shifting Apple from competing projects and departments with separate P&Ls to one single P&L[38] for the entire company.

So whatever your roles are, however you identify yourself: as a venture capitalist, angel investor, fund manager, startup founder, entrepreneur, or business leader, and every other identity you claim; this book is as much about you as a person as it is about business.

Clearly, if you've financial capital in an interest-bearing bank account, invested in startups, public stocks, or in a pension fund, your long term outcomes depend on using the right strategy for the dynamics of your capital.

The only additive dynamic in financial capital most of us ever encounter is earning a monthly salary. But even your monthly salary can have a multiplicative element, because salary increases are usually a percentage of your current salary; promotions, or shifts to a new role or a new company, usually lead to your asking for an increase by some percentage. Equally, if you lose your income, your expenses are likely to be a percentage of your remaining wealth. So again, the multiplicative dynamic. Your personal wealth, salary, and life path is far from ergodic.

If your most important capitals are not financial, apply this book and the ergodic investment strategy to these. How's your reputation? Your self esteem? Your social and relationship capital? All follow the same kind of multiplicative dynamic, one damn thing after another, connected into your life path as it unfolds.

Lawrence Ford AIF, founder of Conscious Capital Wealth Management, Scious, and co-founder of the SDG focussed organisation Future Capital, is also the author of *The Secrets of the Seasons: You're Here for a Reason*[78]. His book is very much about the non-ergodicity of our life paths, the role of beneficial and detrimental unknowables, and how these can trigger developmental growth.

He implicitly puts into practice the non-ergodicity of human life paths, but from traditional rather than mathematical perspectives, which explains why he was called the *Shaman of Wall Street* in a Washington Post article.

Another application to life lies in comparisons. Comparing yourself with somebody else and then judging yourself as better or worse, as successful or not, is at least partially, if not completely flawed, because it's neglecting the non-ergodic nature of your respective paths, and the vitally important role of unpredictables. This is seen very clearly in the research on winning a Nobel prize[30] described in Chapter 1, which showed that beneficial and detrimental unpredictables play a far bigger role in success and failure than innate talent.

This is something that I (Graham) find very helpful to remind myself about.

I'm often very harsh on myself, very readily judging myself as not good enough when I see how far I am from the objectives I've chosen. Sometimes when I find myself comparing myself against others and concluding their successes are because they're better than me, it helps to remind myself to check whether or not that conclusion is supported by robust evidence.

Often all I can say is that their non-ergodic life path currently has more than my non-ergodic life path in the single frame of reference I'm using for this comparison.

And then to remind myself that there are many other frames of reference I could be using.

One of these is using ergodicity and path dependency, not only the current moment, as the frame of reference. I find this extremely helpful: seeing myself as my entire path opens any blinkers created by my current situation or emotional state.

Another frame I find helpful is to recognise all of the beneficial unpredictables that have given me success in my life, in the unique combination and sequence that is mine, and which are not on any other life path in that sequence. The subtitle (*You're Here for a Reason*) of Lawrence's book[78] plus thinking that I am my entire path helps me remember that the reason is in this unique integration.

Unfortunately for those of us who like things known and predictable, most of the time the reason why you are here is an unknowable. As in the story Steve Jobs tells, you can only connect the dots backwards (page 10). You may only see clearly the reason you have been alive right at the end of your life, perhaps not even then; it may take a generation or more before the reason is clear.

I find this helpful in maintaining my balance, especially these days of doom and gloom around the climate, society, the biosphere, and everything else.

The multi-generation non-ergodic nature of life paths also has a key impact on persistent social challenges, and until we can tackle these with ergodic strategies, fully informed by the non-ergodic nature of paths, we will continue to fall short in addressing these challenges. These are the challenges that often end with an 'ism' in their name, and those like multi-generation unemployment, economic inequity, and much more.

Non-ergodicity, and executing an ergodic investment strategy, is also at the core of why diversity and inclusion is worth doing. We need sufficiently large and diverse paths pooling their life capitals.

Whether in an organisation, a society, or any other group, the more diversity there is in life paths the more likely you are to have the diversity you need to benefit from the beneficial and buffer against the detrimental unpredictables that come your way.

Looking at each of our lives as non-ergodic paths, it becomes clear that the real power of diversity in a community is pooling our human capitals (e.g. time, skills, etc., each an independent human capital). In fact, a community (which may be a project team, or the staff as a whole in a business), a tribe, village, etc. is a way of growing and governing a pool of diverse human capitals.

Bernhard Possert, in his programme *The New Good Life*, applies an ergodic strategy to enable his clients to reframe what a good life can be, given the path the world is on.

Climate change, biodiversity loss, planetary boundaries being overshot by most countries, the current industrial revolution driven by the rise of digitisation and AI, etc. mean that the entire concept of the kind of life any of us can aspire towards has fundamentally changed.

Either we adapt, and aspire towards an achievable new good life, or, like the Luddites of the first industrial revolution, we try to arrest change. But we have crossed too many tipping points for any attempt to arrest change to do so. Change has already happened, it is just not yet evenly distributed. We must adapt, and flatten the curve as best possible.

The adaptation framework Possert proposes implicitly has the non-ergodic nature of life at its heart. The key elements of looking at the facts, doing what works now without creating planetary debt for the future, doing together, and accepting that we are nature, are all best executed within an ergodic strategy.

The diverse nature of unpredictables is why you need the widest diversity in human capital pools. For example, young and old cannot replace each other: each life path's current point has strengths and weaknesses. Success in a business, or any other endeavour, needs a diversity of paths in the human capital pool to thrive.

This is at the heart of why collaborating[7] with people you do not agree with, or like, or trust, is essential to achieving breakthroughs in our biggest existential challenges. Exactly the difference between your life path and theirs that prevents you from agreeing, liking, or trusting each other may bring the vital capitals that need to be pooled for each of you to thrive. Hence the benefits of competition (tension / conflict) in collaboration, and vice-versa.

The message is crystal clear: you have the best chance of success for yourself over the next 20 years by being part of a group pooling resources, especially if it has values and intention anchored in creating a viable future, not maintaining the present.

And in some ways that's been the secret of success of all investors: be one of the first investors in the new disruptive technology, not like the last people who bought Kodak shares before the entire photographic film industry collapsed.

Here are some of the key points I (Graham) strive to apply in my life. Not always, not necessarily even very well when I do, but the more I practise, the easier it becomes to apply them, even under stress.

- Luck is important. Avoid evaluations of outcomes according to only skill or talent as a frame of reference; also use different life paths' unpredictables as a frame of reference.

- Pooling resources is important. Build groups of people that you can pool resources with. And govern well; be cautious of becoming one of the few giving into the pool, exclude wisely and gracefully at times.

- Grasp spontaneous opportunities that pop up along your life path, and that you find intriguing, or awaken curiosity in you. One of these may be exactly the unpredictable that, a decade later, turns out to be the reason why you are alive. However, be cautious of only leaping from one new unpredictable to the next, lest you fail to have the discipline to develop it to readiness when you need it a decade later!

CHAPTER 11

Vision: an economy meeting all needs

*"You have been telling people that this is the Eleventh Hour,
now you must go back and tell the people that this is the Hour.
[…]
Then he clasped his hands together, smiled, and said, "This
could be a good time! There is a river flowing now very fast.
It is so great and swift that there are those who will be afraid.
They will try to hold on to the shore. They will feel they are
being torn apart and will suffer greatly. Know the river has
its destination. The elders say we must let go of the shore, push
off into the middle of the river, keep our eyes open, and our
heads above the water.
The time of the lone wolf is over. Gather yourselves! Banish
the word 'struggle' from your attitude and your vocabulary.
All that we do now must be done in a sacred manner and in
celebration.
We are the ones we've been waiting for."*
—Hopi Elders' Prophecy

By now I hope you are beginning to imagine that businesses can achieve outcomes that have so far seemed hard or even impossible, if it uses ergodic strategies. In this chapter I'll tell a story of one future we might have through the potential of ergodic strategies.

This is one scenario. There are many scenarios, each differentiated by which unpredictables occur in which sequence. And, most importantly, by our choice of strategy. Do we execute a fully ergodic strategy across our global economy; or not.

The tipping points to this vision, or to any of the other visions that humanity's path could follow, are themselves unpredictables. Because of this, the rational strategy is acceptance of unpredictables as an invitation to keep doing everything we can in innovative ways, investing our time, money, and other capitals, according to ergodic investment strategies.

Imagine you've just woken up after having been cryogenically frozen for half a century. You've thawed out, had a shower, eaten your favourite breakfast, and have just dressed in your favourite clothing.

Now you're wondering why your favourite breakfast and clothing are still available! Maybe this means that the world in 2073 is a much better place than you had feared it would become when you were frozen in 2023.

You ask the people taking care of your re-entry to life what the world outside is like. They tell you: "It's a world built so that all needs can be met, and where, regardless of the starting point of your life path, you experience the world as a just and equitable place[81]. After all," they say, "any other strategy is a strategy choosing to fail someone."

"How did we get here?" you ask.

The shorter one replies: "Once we had fully understood what it meant to live in an unpredictable world with primarily multiplicative non-ergodic dynamics driving changes in all of the capitals, we quickly rebuilt the economy and the larger society according to ergodic strategies, taking us closer to the ergodic limit. This was a key enabler in eliminating capital wastage in each of the six capitals, and living within our planetary boundaries.

"Crucial to getting there: we stopped clinging to the safe shore of our old dysfunctional beliefs and institutions. We gave up our futile attempts to create certainty, and instead accepted the inherent unpredictables of life, embraced feeling insecure and unsafe. This enabled us to ride the inexorable river of change, as per the prophecy[82] of the Hopi Elders. It very quickly became clear to everyone that clinging any longer to the collapsing shore would eventually leave us high and dry with nothing."

Their taller colleague picks up the tale, saying: "Once we'd fully understood that the time expectation of each of our paths, even seen from the purely selfish perspective, was maximised if we all followed an ergodic strategy, it was the investors, entrepreneurs, and others well-versed in strategies for maximising wealth that led the way.

"Because it was better for them, they quickly built businesses designed for blended competition and collaboration outside the forced compromise line, for multi-capital pooling mechanisms using currencies native to each capital.

"Then a range of early adopters and middle majority from all walks of life joined in, after seeing that innovative investors and entrepreneurs were now more successful for themselves because their actions benefited nature and society. This kick-started a positive feedback loop that accelerated everything.

"More and more people saw a believable alternative to the historical paradigm, where only one in twelve startups[83] was ultimately fully successful for investors and entrepreneurs. Now, businesses that were most likely to grow did grow, and most of the value of those that shut down stayed in the ecosystem, delivering returns through the other businesses. In this new way of working, everyone's actions led to better outcomes with less cost, effort, and stress."

You begin to realise that the true nature of business was not what everyone had thought it was. You begin to see the implications of each individual business actually being a single path, from first inception to final demise.

What once had been an effortful struggle to force individual businesses to be net positive, regenerative, sustainable, circular, doughnut, etc. now happened out of self-interest as a natural consequence of excellently executed ergodic strategies. These good changes naturally emerged in an ergodic investment strategy across all six capitals.

"Are you saying, we realised that the maps business had been using to navigate by were flawed, and the lenses we'd built to see the territory clearly were instead distorting it?" you ask.

"Yes," said the taller of the two, "that's exactly it.

"Once people saw that the problem lay with the maps and lenses they were using, not with themselves, a wave of grounded optimism and energy began building. More and more dived into this new blue ocean of business that profitably benefited society and the environment, creating completely new kinds of businesses, and new ways of doing business, that harnessed as a strength all of the unpredictables, from known through to unknowable.

"The business community, civil society, and government made distortion-free lenses and true maps[1].

"It was a bit like the old video[2] of people joining in a dance on the side of a hill. As you see, the first person started dancing alone, the first follower joined in, creating the seed of a community others aspired to belong to, and soon everyone was dancing. What really made the difference was the first follower, not the person dancing alone.

"In the beginning," they concluded, "there was no universal agreement on what the solution was, but everyone agreed that we needed a breakthrough, that we needed local and global economies that did a good job of getting all needs met. It was enough to agree that change was needed, and accept a diversity of directions and solutions."

Now you saw that humanity had achieved that change far more rapidly than you had imagined possible in 2023.

All we had needed to do was remove the blocks preventing each of us, and business as a whole, from fully expressing our true nature: individual paths in a non-ergodic world of multiplicative unpredictables. Which led to us developing many different ways of building business and our lives to explore the mystery of what we could do with the unpredictables, instead of trying to prevent them from happening[3].

You remembered, in the years before you had decided to be cryogenically frozen, how many of your friends could not see any way of cleaning up the mess we had created. You remembered how many simply continued with their lives, or even actively resisted change.

You remembered reading Michael A. Singer's words in his book *The Surrender Experiment*[1]:

> *Challenging situations create the force needed to bring about*
> *change. The problem is that we generally use all the stirred up*

---

[1] You'll find DIY details on map-making and lens-building in *Rebuild*[6].

[2] First follower video; how new movements begin: https://www.youtube.com/watch?v=fW8amMCVAJQ

[3] This is the focus of a working group I've been leading under the auspices of Future Capital[84], which Lawrence Ford was asked to start by the UN SDG unit.

energy, intended to bring about change, to resist change; or at least passively ignore it.

I was learning to sit quietly in the midst of the howling winds and wait to see what constructive action was being asked of me.

The taller one spoke again, bringing you back out of your memories of your thoughts and experiences in the years before your freezing.

"As in the words of the Hopi prophecy stating that *'this could be a good time!'* people began to accept that the opportunity to be part of creating the kind of world we now have was beyond a once-in-a-lifetime opportunity; it was a once in a millennium opportunity! Everything was changing. What was coming were unpredictables: a few were known unpredictables, most were unknown or even unknowable."

"Two big known unpredictables were when we would cross the 1.5C rise, and when the Greenland ice sheet would completely melt. Comparing what has happened in the geological past and what was happening in 2023, it was clear that it would melt far faster than our linear minds want to imagine[85]. But, we reasoned that if we acted fast and big to transform our economy to a net positive economy, using a powerfully ergodic strategy, we could prevent complete melt-down.

"Enough people finally fully appreciated that we humans had caused a complete transformation of the biosphere, which was driving a complete transformation of human society, which was driving a complete transformation of society's economy. More and more of us realised that resisting this transformation was about as intelligent as King Canute resisting the tide[4].

"Step-by-step, people realised that the time to surrender to the transformation had come. It was the hour. They understood that surrender didn't just mean 'give up and let it roll over us'. Nor did it mean checking out of life, or society, or business. Instead surrender was invigorating, driving change, because it enabled us to use all of the energy in the transformation.

---

[4]Which, apparently, was not his intent; his intent was to demonstrate to his court the futility of resisting inevitable change, instead that even the king must accept the invitations of inexorable change.

"We finally let go of all of our attempts to eliminate the unpredictables and saw clearly how, in every previous civilisation, refusing to let go of the shore of illusory predictability had led to the collapse of all earlier civilisations[25].

"So we embraced the unpredictables that came our way, knowing that only by doing so would we have the best chance of our ergodic strategy leading to benefits from the upside of all of the unpredictables. After all, we realised, if it has worked from the birth of life on our planet, perhaps it is the best proven strategy for success of the human subset of all life.

"Of course this was far from harmonious agreement across 8 billion people on everything. We could never have done it without the big insight that striving for everyone to agree as a precursor to collaboration was dysfunctional. In fact, we needed arguments and tensions, we needed to keep multiple different opinions and perspectives behind those tensions, to execute a sufficiently powerful ergodic strategy.

"Nor did we all agree on one right path. But because we'd learnt enough about unpredictables, unknowables, and non-ergodic path-dependent outcomes, we did agree on just enough to collaborate[7], even with people who disliked, disagreed with, and even mistrusted each other.

"All that was agreed was that the current state was untenable, and that we could get somewhere better—even if we couldn't agree on exactly what was wrong today, nor where that somewhere better was—by each taking one step in a direction that they thought was promising, comparing notes, pooling lucky wins, and then repeating.

"And there was enough agreement that the future of business ought not be built on a fantasy, but according to its true non-ergodic nature.

"Fortunately we had many excellent transformational facilitators, like Adam Kahane, adept at enabling collaboration between natural enemies. People who understood that much of what really mattered was unknowable, unpredictable, a mystery. Who understood that creating a better world required, as Kahane wrote, 'removing everything blocking the mystery from expressing itself fully'[48].

"As in nature, once an ecosystem is not prevented from growing according to its essence, the most effective ecosystem will grow. All we needed to do was remove the barriers. This gave us the necessary tools to do what some economists, such as Peter Söderbaum[86], had been saying, on how to achieve sustainability.

"After understanding that the true nature of business would effortlessly express itself if we stopped blocking it, and that this true nature was both better for each of us individually and better for all of us collectively, we took the first steps."

"What were they, and what have they led to?" you ask.

"These are the first steps we took to remove the blocks. You'll see that everything becomes easy once you remove everything blocking necessary interactions and flows from flowing.

- We incorporated startups as a commons[6], inclusive of all the capitals they touched, and all the primary stakeholders they interacted with. Governance and wealth was equitably shared across all capitals and stakeholders. And pooled.

- We invested in entire and highly diverse startup ecosystems via holding companies, instead of directly in each startup. And the holding companies themselves included all capitals and stakeholders. Then the pooling and requisite diversity became effortless.

- In addition to money we used multiple complementary currencies defined according to the essence of their associated capital. Such as the Japanese time currency, the Fureai Kippu, the Swiss WIR currency (CHW).

- And so each business ecosystem began to multiply all six capitals, instead of being an exchange mechanism from the non-financial capitals into financial capital, with a needlessly high transaction cost that prevented business from being sustainable.

- Within each business, we used fluid organisation designs like Sociocracy and Holacracy, making it fast and effortless for the business to respond to the unpredictables as they emerged.

- And everybody integrated these fluid organisation designs with structured ways of interacting with each other, like the Adaptive Way[6], so that each person could clearly identify their own essence by using their internal conflict and conflict with others as a lens. The same patterns then also allowed people to interact within teams in ways that enabled effortless joint action, because rather than blocking each other's essence they enabled the essence of each to be maximally productive. Most importantly, this enabled us to work with unpredictables despite our preference for predictability and safety.

"So by doing all this you now have an economy that actually does its job, provisioning for all life on Earth? One that is naturally net positive because the essence of each capital is working in positive complicity with the essence of all other capitals, each multiplying each? Because of this, all the Sustainable Development Goals were achieved, including the capacity of the planet's biosphere to support all life, including human life?" you asked.

"Yes!" they both replied in unison.

"Of course," the shorter added, "this does not mean that everybody is going around in a trance of bliss, with everything flat and equal. Just as in nature there is a full diversity of human beings and life paths. Only now in a dynamic balance that works far better for everyone.

"Each business itself is fully recognised as a free non-human legal person, a commons of productive capacity, where the stakeholders, and especially the stewards, act like the guardians of a human being that lacks the capacity to communicate unaided.

"Every business is connected with other businesses around it, using resource pooling across all capitals. Because of this, businesses are created, thrive, and die away. They may die because they are attacked by a predator, or they may die because they reach the natural end of their lifespan. But however they die, nothing is lost to the economy. All the capital wealth they have grown in each of the six capitals remains part of the ecosystem because the pooling and the flow brings the whole ecosystem close to the ergodic maximum expected outcome. This is full fiduciary responsibility: all capitals are not just preserved, but grown."

"Equally important, zombie businesses, those on life support because someone doesn't want to let them die, are hospiced and helped to die with dignity," the taller one added.

"When unpredictables lead certain businesses to thrive, the businesses around them share in that bounty, thriving too, just as you see in nature: when a spring and summer with an optimum balance of rain and sun creates a surfeit of plant growth, the animals sharing that bounty thrive, and this thriving life breaks more rock down, deepening the soils, and generally setting that natural ecosystem up to do even better in coming seasons.

Even those lacking in rainfall. The same in our economy, financial abundance now increases the entire planet's capacity to sustain life, rather than decreasing it the way it used to.

"Inventors and founders with a superb intuition for what's needed are able to build businesses, regardless of their historical life path, because of resource pooling. Whether your life path has many sequences of beneficial unpredictables or not, you have enough access to the resource pool to at least have a good chance of demonstrating how your idea adds value to the global economy.

"And if not," said the shorter one, "you will get quick and clear feedback that this idea doesn't work, just as nature gives quick and clear feedback to any new species that is a poor fit to the needs of nature as a whole.

"People, and businesses, that do not agree with, like, or even trust each other are still able to collaborate[7] and compete in ways that continuously strengthen local and global economies over the long haul."

"There are no longer businesses that are like an amoeba scaling to the size of an elephant. No single business is the sole global provider of some essential service for the functioning of the ecosystem.

"Rather, we have a wide variety of different businesses and a wide range of different business sizes.

"Because of this, each has a different exposure to the unpredictables on their paths, each hits good luck and bad luck at different times, with different cycle times; and so all of them together, with an appropriate level of resource pooling, have an expected outcome close to the ergodic maximum.

"Each business, and the economy as a whole, fully embraces the value and necessity of power. The power to get things done, to create, to change," added the taller one.

"Drive, enthusiasm, anger, and conflict show up; but as a complementary pair with the capacity to come together, to work together in harmony, to be together in oneness. Connection, caring, altruism, and shared joy show up.

"Overall there is justice. Not a static justice where nothing harmful happens, but a dynamic justice where harmful things do happen, and then the structures and interactions restore a just equilibrium[7,48].

"And economists now talk about the velocity of all capitals in a confluence, rather than just the velocity of money. They talk about how much of each capital is flowing with what velocity, in what kind of confluence with which other capitals are flowing, with what velocity. We created a confluence of capitals that made the impossible normal, just like Hercules did with the Augean stables."

"I remember clearly," said the shorter one, "the words my gran Marie told my mom when she was just eight, to describe what she was doing, as a pioneer in building business ecosystems according to the ergodic investment strategy:

> *We're building businesses with people who love the planet and their children, and want to protect and rebuild all life on earth, while being fair to everyone.*"

"I get it!," you exclaim. "We've finally understood that the essence of business is not the same as the constructs we've built to express that essence. In fact, the constructs of the 400 years before I was frozen actually distorted the essence of business, preventing it from doing its job of providing for all, prevented it from being net positive across all capitals. Now we build constructs to fully express the essence of business: the fundamental tool to provision for all, across all capitals, in a non-ergodic world dominated by unpredictables."

CHAPTER 12

Conclusion

*I am one of those who think like Nobel, that humanity will
draw more good than evil from new discoveries.*
—Marie Curie

In the preface I invited you, every time you read something different to your truth, to at least rent the idea for a while. To ask yourself some questions enabling you to look back at where your truth came from, in order to compare it, and the experiences in your past that created it, with what you were reading.

How has it been?

Perhaps you recognise that the time is ripe for disruptive innovation, and that ergodic strategies may well be a crucial pillar of that disruption. Will you accept the invitation to start using ergodic strategies?

I invite you to join us in looking at your investment and business results as an expression of the non-ergodic equations that describe real world capital change processes.

Perhaps you're sure that nothing in this book is true, or at least nothing can ever be put into practise. Perhaps you're neither sure what to make of the book nor your current approach to investing and business building. Perhaps uncomfortable anomalies that you've been experiencing over the years snapped into clarity as you read this book, and you realised it was time to get rid of some of the foundations of your current approach as an investor or entrepreneur. But you'll stay as you are for a while yet—after all, it's working well for you, and change is challenging.

If you're hesitating, think of a time in your past where some major transformation happened in your life. One where you resisted initially, but once you had experienced what it brought you, you have never gone back to the old way. I'm now inviting you to rent the idea just a little bit longer to put an ergodic strategy into practice and taste what it can bring you.

Try out the idea that unpredictables are a bigger part of life than you've believed so far. That all we can control is how we respond to these unpredictables when they emerge. That our best bet is to build an ecosystem according to an ergodic investment strategy that generates the maximum in beneficial outcomes and the minimum in detrimental outcomes.

Maybe something in your philosophy of life doesn't fit well with this book. It fits well with mine, because my personal meaning-making is that much is one unpredictable after another, lacking any deeper meaning in the pattern. Staying sceptical of any meaning, because it may well be imposing my meaning into randomness, not a real pattern.

You might have a completely different meaning-making. You might see Adam Smith's invisible hand in the unpredictables; you might see them as the expression of God's mystery; you might see them all as life's plan, or as your karmic destiny. Whichever meaning you make, the constant across all of these meaning-making stories is that for each of us here and now, the future is filled with unpredictables that we cannot predict with certainty, even if we use all the available tools, knowledge, and money.

For most of us, fully understanding and executing an ergodic strategy is an adaptive challenge: one that requires first changing our beliefs. Which requires adaptive capacity, described in Part 3 of Rebuild[6]. And a lack of adaptive capacity is why we have a track record of stubbornly holding beliefs in the face of overwhelming evidence that it's time to change them!

The investment choices you make today are in connected paths of unpredictables. Fiduciary responsibility applies to financial and all other capitals, and it requires acting in ways that grow all of the capitals. This means accepting that the unpredictables are there, that the paths connecting these unpredictables have a non-ergodic multiplicative wealth dynamic, and that your investment strategy is more likely to be successful if it is ergodic.

And this is true for your financial wealth, your intellectual wealth, your relationship wealth, and your self-esteem, as well as the natural capital wealth of the natural world around you.

It means that, when you wake each day, you have no idea what the companies that you've invested in are going to put on your desk. But if you're following an ergodic investment strategy, there's no need to know. Your job is simply to do your best with whatever happens to increase the capacity of the entire ecosystem to approach the maximum outcome set by the ergodic limit, regardless of personal preferences[24].

You can think of the ergodic limit in capital growth processes as akin to the speed of light in physical processes: you can never expect to do better than that. If you do, it's actually not your doing, rather a lucky throw of the die. Fiduciary responsibility means your job is, every day, to increase your capacity to approach the ergodic limit, in other words, increase your capacity to systemically embrace the opportunities unpredictables bring your way.

The better all of us can do this, starting today, (remember, this is the hour, the 11th hour was a decade ago), the better the position we're each in to do the job in front of us: to do our part in building an economy capable of providing for the needs of our society, which requires regenerating the biosphere providing much of what we need to live.

A growing community of individuals across the spectrum has grasped that business has been navigating according to a distorted map, built on the flawed assumption that capital processes are ergodic. Now that we know that they are not ergodic, and that the way we are building our economy and each individual business is maximising the detrimental consequences of non-ergodic business processes, it's time for each of us, regardless of how we're involved in our economy, to join together in navigating and guiding what we do by using ergodic investment strategies that take us as close as possible to the ergodic limit.

Whether you are driven by maximising financial returns for your limited partners; maximising impact or philanthropic outcomes in non-financial, or even all capitals; feeling good doing what you love; or leaving a legacy; your best bet is an ergodic investment strategy. And that will naturally lead to Marie's vision (page 125) because it is at its most powerful when all capitals and stakeholders are part of its execution.

Today's business paradigm has run out of road. More and more investors, entrepreneurs, and business leaders are already coming together around business and investment paradigms, such as net positive, regenerative, impact, climate, conscious capitalism, circular economy, and much more. Each of these has common ground with the others, and valuable uniqueness of its own. We need all of them.

All of these are part of the new nature of business. And each is already a nascent ergodic strategy.

The future is already here; it's just poorly distributed and insufficiently visible.

As more and more people join us in recognising that the true nature of business is the non-ergodic, path-dependent, multiplicative dynamics of all capitals, more of us will have better success in our roles as investors, entrepreneurs, etc., because we are all individually and collectively best served by ergodic strategies.

Ultimately we need ergodic finance, underpinned by ergodicity economics, as the foundation for everything we do as investors and entrepreneurs.

Let's close the circle now, and integrate competence and luck into one complementary pair. Starting with Occam's Razor:

> *The simplest explanation, with the fewest assumptions, is most likely the right explanation.*

Or as Einstein put it,

> *Everything should be kept as simple as possible, but not simpler.*

This leads to Hanlon's Razor:

> *Never attribute to malice that which is adequately explained by stupidity.*

I now propose the Ergodic Razor:

> *Attribute to no other cause that which is adequately explained by non-ergodic dynamics and unpredictables.*

After the ergodic razor, all of your personal strengths, such as skill, wisdom, dialectic fluidity, and perseverance; and around you all the systemic organisational strengths, including strategy, contingency planning, organisational resilience, and competence; make all the difference in tilting the outcomes in your favour.

When detrimental unpredictables emerge, the better your own dialectic fluidity[6] (ability to see options for success by using thought forms beyond simple linear logic), the better your skill in surfing unpredictables, the stronger your perseverance to keep going until a beneficial unpredictable turns everything around, the more likely you are to be in the game and successful at the end.

The bigger your wisdom in seeing clearly the interwoven role of unpredictables and your qualities in your success or failure, the better your long-term chances.

I (Graham) had a friend in South Africa who, discovering that she was pregnant after breaking up with her partner, created a way of making being a single mum work for her. She opened a nursery, quickly added another 30 paying children to her daughter, and hired a team of nannies to take care of them all. Leaving her with more free time than before, and more joyful time with her daughter.

This is an ergodic strategy in action: resource pooling with other mothers so that all individually have more time and a better quality of life for themselves and their children.

As Gary Player popularised: *'Lucky? Yes, I've been lucky in my golf; and you know what, the harder I practise, the luckier I get!'*

At the end of the day, we're all exposed to good and bad fortune, events outside our circle of control. Success is about using the best ergodic strategy to harness fortune, developing the skills to execute it with excellence, and the wisdom to tell the difference[1].

Luck is not a strategy—except when it's ergodic!

[1]Riffing off the Serenity Prayer commonly attributed to Reinhold Niebuhr and perhaps first articulated by Winnifred Crane Wygal

Acknowledgements

Graham

Everything that you have read in this book has come out of my understanding of what works, based on my experiences over five decades, including what I have learnt from many more able than I am. These have been shaped and informed by countless others; people I have known in person, people I have known through others, and people I have never met who have written books or given superb talks.

Much of this has been shaped by my early life in South Africa, the privileges I had growing up there, and my amazingly supporting parents. My late father, Hylton, my mother, Barbara, and my sister Tessa, have all contributed an unknowably large contribution to me being me, and this book bringing you whatever value you have taken from it. My work today is in part driven by a desire to pay forward to the next generations all the good things that previous generations, and the beneficial context I was lucky to be born into, have given me.

I was also privileged to go to excellent schools, Selborne Primary and College, and then to the excellent Universities of Cape Town and Bielefeld. I cannot know how my life would have turned out without everything I learnt there, both about subjects and about life, from my peers and teachers. These changed the path my life would otherwise have taken.

There are a few though who have been important contributors to this book itself. The co-founders of Evolutesix, especially Marie-Nicole Arbelias Schuster and Nikyta Guleria have played a key role in refining the development of the FairShares Commons and our ergodic investment strategy. And Magdalena Schäffer, for developing with me the tools, applications, and stories to bring this to life.

Prof. Rory Ridley-Duff and colleagues, who's FairShares I integrated with my Free / Commons Company approach.

Otto Laske's seminal work on the Cognitive Developmental Framework has been the theoretical foundation for much of my own development over the past decade, and hence for Evolutesix and this book.

Paraphrasing Newton, if you are benefitting from this book, it is because I have benefitted from standing on the shoulders of giants.

Eva Gottschlich has been very generous in her support in making this book possible, for which I will always be grateful.

There are many more that have contributed significantly yet have not been mentioned by name; you'll know if you have contributed, and I thank you! However long I make this section, I will still be missing some important people.

Jack

Writing the acknowledgements is both humbling and surprisingly arduous, since it forces one to realize that a book is never the product of one (or two) people) but the culmination of many. I am able to write this book because of who I am. I am who I am because of who my parents were, my grandparents, and their parents before them. I am who I am because I was born and raised in Norwood, Massachusetts. I am who I am because I attended a fine college prep school, Xaverian, in Westwood Massachusetts; then attended a superior liberal arts college, Holy Cross, in Worcester Massachusetts. I am who I am because I earned my doctorate in economics from the University of Notre Dame in Notre Dame, Indiana.

Change any one of these and I would not be the person I am today, and needless to say, I wouldn't have been able to write this book. It is too general (and meaningless) to acknowledge everyone I've ever been in contact with, yet arrogantly misleading to mention no one. Unfortunately, no recipe exists for how to choose and select. Perhaps best is to acknowledge individuals from the different stages of my life.

First and foremost, my grandfather, Lester Reardon, who first taught me about sustainability and the future of the world, back when no one gave it much thought. My high school American Literature teacher, Brother Joe

Girard who taught me the art of writing, the alluring appeal of good literature, and that to be a good writer one must be an artist, and that to be an artist, one must be a wordsmith. At Holy Cross, Professor Frank Petrella, whose economics classes I couldn't get enough of, steered me into economics, as well as to Notre Dame, his alma mater. At Notre Dame, I thank the Economics Admissions Committee (Charles Wilber, Larry Marsh, and Charles Craypo) for taking a chance on me, especially after confessing in my application essay that I was writing a novel (which for some in economics is an anathema). I am happy to report that my novel *Swimming Backwards* was published in 2022 (finally) and that I am working on a second one.

To my students (too legion to mention individually) who motivate me every day to do my best to educate and not to proselytize, who have shown me that education is our most important investment and that to teach is to engage in a noble profession.

And finally, to my children Elizabeth and Patrick, who have taught me so much, and whose lives are forever intertwined with mine. Someday, I can only hope that they will say that not only was I a great father, and a good friend, and a fine role model, but that I worked and taught and wrote to give our generation the needed tools to lead sustainable and productive lives.

Overall book

Both of us are enormously grateful to a number of people who have contributed to making this book possible. Anna Kierstan, our editor, has achieved the challenge of polishing all our rough edges away.

We would both like to thank everyone, especially Odyssey and Phillis, at Granny Dot's near Tzaneen in South Africa, who took such excellent care of us at various stages of writing our books. The people and the place proved a vital source of inspiration, both when we were there, and in our memories afterwards.

This book was also made possible by support in cash and in kind by the following people, both through our crowdfunding campaign, and directly.

12.1 Backers

We also very much appreciate the financial backing enabling us to complete this book from the following people.

Ergodium

- Phillipe Schmidig

Gold

- Bernhard Possert

Silver

- Pascale Hazeleger
- Thomas Haas

Bronze

- Robbie Stamp

About the authors

Graham

I (Graham) began working on ergodic and non-ergodic questions in my early 20s, working as a university researcher in particle physics, using path integrals to calculate the properties of fundamental particles at ultrahigh temperatures. My physics career culminated in the research I did using what was then the world's fastest supercomputer, the CP-PACS at the then Center for Computational Physics of Tsukuba University, north of Tokyo.

I then joined Procter & Gamble, and naturally I continued to use the lenses and patterns of thought I'd learnt in physics. After all, once you've learnt to use a range of lenses to see, you only add new, more sophisticated lenses; you do not lose the lenses you have.

Over the next 10 years, time and again I saw particles, interactions, connected together in a path with multiplicative properties. Few of my colleagues saw the connectivity and relatedness that I was seeing; few saw the cause and effect sequence that is obvious when you look through the lens of "connected, ordered paths", simply because they had different lenses, better for seeing other things.

I left Procter & Gamble in 2008, driven by seeing the climate and biosphere crisis so clearly, and my inability to effect meaningful change within the boundaries of business as usual. And committed to rebuilding business to express its essence perfectly: a means of growing and distributing capitals in general (not just money). This can only be achieved by building businesses fully respecting the non-ergodic essence of life. And recognising that the essence of life itself is an autopoietic means of growing and distributing the capitals life itself depends on.

I began by co-founding a building integrated photovoltaics company, moved on to a leadership development and learning transfer company, a think and do tank, and in 2012 began offering as a consultant what is now in this book and in Rebuild[6].

While it was in some sense navigating by looking at everything as connected paths, that both competition and collaborative resource pooling in an optimised blend was the best success strategy, every year I better understood what that meant and how to do it well. The final "aha moment" of clarity, the formal maths underpinning what I was doing, came when I read Ole Peters' work in 2019. Then I could see clearly the lens I'd been using. Even now, every year brings a deeper understanding of what life being non-ergodic really means in practice, for individual lives, for business, and for life as a whole.

Growing up in apartheid South Africa has shaped other lenses I use. Lenses seeing inequity, injustices, doing my best to address them; and seeing clearly how the postcode lottery of where you're born biases against certain life paths. All of these uncontrollable unpredictables, and a few that I was able to influence—living and working in Germany, Italy, Japan, Belgium, China, and the UK in that sequence—are core to my personal life path, which has led me to what I'm doing now.

Jack

Few of us would want to live a fully scripted life; to know not only how it ends, but every twist and turn. For what makes life interesting and fulfilling is the richness of the twists, the uncontrollable unpredictables along one's path.

To paraphrase the movie *The Matrix*, if I were offered the choice of one pill to know every avenue and twist and turn of my life, and another pill to know nothing but the current day, I would without hesitation take the latter. Not knowing beforehand who I would meet and fall in love with; not knowing who my children would be and the individuals they would become; not knowing the books that I would write, and even the friends I would meet who would eventually co-author books with me.

Uncontrollable unpredictables have played a profound role in my life (in addition to being a central theme of this book). Not only altering my life course and making me into a different person but multiplicatively rein-forcing each other. Here's one example: After I received my doctorate in Economics from Notre Dame, I was leading a Kuhnian academic existence writing journal articles to nudge the discipline forward. But one of my art-icles purported to challenge and impugn the very foundation of economics.

Somewhat optimistic that the published article would be heralded as taking economics in a new direction I was shocked when the journal ed-itor tersely admonished, "How dare you!" It was then—a late January after-noon—when I had an epiphany that we needed a new journal in econom-ics, one that fostered and nurtured the ability (and willingness) to criticize, to dialogue, and to challenge. After reading (and re-reading) the letter, I literally flipped it over and sketched out a new journal in economics edu-cation—the International Journal of Pluralism and Economics Education (IJPEE). Two years later (in 2009) the IJPEE it was up and running, and 14 years later, it is still going strong.

The IJPEE has opened up a lot of doors me by introducing me to won-derful people all over the world, committed to reconceptualizing econom-ics and economics education. In 2014, for example, I was invited to present at an MBA teaching conference at the University of Science and Techno-logy of China, in Hefei, where I became fast friends with Lu Wei. During a free-afternoon mountain event, I met and became good friends with Prithvi Yadav, at that time, teaching in Kanpur, India. After the Conference both individuals invited me numerous time to lecture and teach, and I likewise them to the USA. And while in India I also met (by chance) Awadh Dubey, an eye surgeon, living in Kanpur, dedicated to helping India's poor. Today, these three are amongst my closest friends, each reinforcing my passion to educate, to help the less fortunate, and to make the world just and sustain-able.

Thanks to my work with the IJPEE and the books on economics edu-cation that I was writing, I became active with the nascent Rethinking Eco-nomics, a student led organization dedicated to reconceptualizing econom-ics and economics education. Presenting a paper at a conference in London, Graham Boyd had asked a question (a provocatively thoughtful one at that) which I did my best to answer. We continued our conversation afterwards, realizing that we shared the same values and the same desire to write a book. This chance meeting led to the writing of Rebuild and to this book (and several more books in the near-future).

Another uncontrollable unpredictable that I feel compelled to mention: In 1990, I took a group of my students to what was then the Soviet Union—a fascinating yet logistically daunting country to visit. One our stops was in Riga, Latvia, where I had arranged an informal visit for my students with students at Latvia University. Students quickly paired up, leaving me alone. Bored, I ventured out and entered a building that looked promising (office lights were on). In a hallway, I heard several men arguing in Latvian, their voices seemingly escalating as I got closer. Curious, I peered through the half- open door. One professor sizing me up, looked at my shoes, and knowing that I was an American, asked me if I played basketball. (It turned out that they were one player short for an important game, and without him, they would have to forfeit.) Yes, I replied, for back then I was a decent player who could hold his own on the court. After the game, I was invited to return to campus to lecture. A lecture that extended into numerous invites over the next ten years, as well as a chance meeting with the dean of the newly formed ISM University in Vilnius, Lithuania, which led to more teaching invites. All this brought about by one curious wandering—an uncontrollable unpredictable if there ever was one.

And finally, one more. I met my wife on a blind date. It was one of those magical moments that one reads in romance novels (well, some of us). And yes, we fell in love, and yes, we got married, and yes, we had children and raised a family.

I am who I am because of these unpredictables. To understand why I wrote this book is to know who I am. And to understand who I am is to understand how unpredictables have affected me, sometimes nudging me forward and sometimes backwards, but always in a new direction, sometimes even on a new path.

I am fortunate to teach economics at the University of Wisconsin-Eau Claire, a thriving liberal arts college about 90 miles due east of Minneapolis. When I'm not teaching, I'm editing the IJPPE, and when I am not editing, I'm working on books with Graham, and when I'm not working on our books, I'm working on a second novel. Cooking at home, and traveling relaxes me.

About Evolutesix

Evolutesix is an ecosystem holding company and venture builder, incubator, and accelerator, creating and scaling new startups, and transforming existing startups and mature businesses, all according to our Adaptive Organisation Methodology, following an ergodic strategy.

In addition, Evolutesix provides workshops for investors, founders, and leaders on how to create and execute their own ergodic investment strategy; and to everyone who wants to bring this into their personal life path.

Evolutesix is actively accelerating the application of ergodicity in business because it is the missing link for business to really do the job that life asks of it: provisioning across all needs, all capitals, for all lifeforms. This is part of the job that life expects humans to do, and business is a tool we've invented to do this.

The driver for Evolutesix is the recognition that our polycrises of climate change, resource depletion, biosphere collapse, and many more, require multisolving—finding single systemic actions that solve multiple problems. Such multisolutions require new, inherently net positive structures for investments and businesses, which will lead to a viable economy for a viable future for humanity. And that if we do this too slowly, the polycrises will end badly for all of us.

Contact us if you want to know more about our offers to investors, entrepreneurs, and individuals, or as keynote speakers at your event, via our website evolutesix.com.

More information about us, this book, and our earlier book *Rebuild: the Economy, Leadership, and You* is at graham-boyd.biz

Bibliography

[1] M.A. Singer. *The Surrender Experiment: My Journey Into Life's Perfection*. Hodder & Stoughton.

[2] Nassim Nicholas Taleb. *Skin in the Game: Hidden Asymmetries in Daily Life*. Random House.

[3] Julie Segal. URL: https://www.institutionalinvestor.com/article/b1nhg4w9k5hjp0/Nassim-Taleb-and-Universa-Versus-the-World (visited on 30/03/2023).

[4] Joanna Glasner. 'The Biggest Startup IPOs Of The Past 10 Years Are All Below Their First-Day Price'. In: (9th May 2023). URL: https://news.crunchbase.com/public/venture-backed-us-startups-ipos/ (visited on 12/05/2023).

[5] J.F. Moore. *The Death of Competition: Leadership and Strategy in the Age of Business Ecosystems*. HarperBusiness.

[6] G. Boyd and J. Reardon. *Rebuild: the Economy, Leadership, and You*. Evolutesix Books.

[7] A. Kahane. *Collaborating with the Enemy: How to Work with People You Don't Agree with or Like or Trust*. Berrett-Koehler Publishers. ISBN: 9781626568228.

[8] Mark Buchanan. *How ergodicity reimagines economics for the benefit of us all*. URL: https://aeon.co/amp/ideas/how-ergodicity-reimagines-economics-for-the-benefit-of-us-all.

[9] P. Polman and A. Winston. *Net Positive: How Courageous Companies Thrive by Giving More Than They Take*. Harvard Business Review Press. ISBN: 9781647821319.

[10] K. Schwab and P. Vanham. *Stakeholder Capitalism: A Global Economy that Works for Progress, People and Planet*. Wiley.

[11] John Fullerton. *Regenerative Capitalism, the Capital Institute*. URL: https://capitalinstitute.org/regenerative-capitalism/ (visited on 21/11/2022).

[12] Daniel Christian Wahl. *Designing Regenerative Cultures*. Triarchy Press.

[13] L.H. Lovins et al. *A Finer Future: Creating an Economy in Service to Life*. New Society Publishers.

[14] John Elkington. *25 Years Ago I Coined the Phrase "Triple Bottom Line." Here's Why It's Time to Rethink It*. 25th June 2018.

[15] *Ellen MacArthur Foundation publications on the Circular Economy*. URL: https://ellenmacarthurfoundation.org/publications (visited on 21/11/2022).

[16] Gunter Pauli. *The blue economy, a report to the Club of Rome*. URL: https://www.theblueeconomy.org/.

[17] John Mackey and Rajendra Sisodia. *Conscious Capitalism, With a New Preface by the Authors: Liberating the Heroic Spirit of Business*. Harvard Business Review Press.

[18] *B-Corp*. URL: https://www.bcorporation.net/ (visited on 21/11/2022).

[19] Purpose Foundation. *Steward Ownership*. URL: https://purpose-economy.org/.

[20] Alex Pazaitis, Michel Bauwens and Vasilis Kostakis. *Peer to Peer: The Commons Manifesto*. University of Westminster Press.

[21] Martin P. Thomas and Mark W McElroy. URL: https://www.multicapitalscorecard.com/.

[22] *Regens Unite*. URL: https://www.regensunite.earth/ (visited on 21/11/2022).

[23] Elizabeth Sawin. *Climate Interactive*. URL: https://www.climateinteractive.org/programs/multisolving/what-is-multisolving/ (visited on 14/11/2022).

[24] D. McRaney. *How Minds Change: The New Science of Belief, Opinion and Persuasion.* Oneworld Publications.

[25] Jared Diamond. *Collapse: How Societies Choose to Fail or Succeed.* Penguin, New York.

[26] URL: https://companiesmarketcap.com/procter-and-gamble/marketcap/ (visited on 08/11/2022).

[27] URL: https://companiesmarketcap.com/zoom/marketcap/ (visited on 08/11/2022).

[28] URL: https://www.crunchbase.com/organization/getyourguide/company_financials (visited on 08/11/2022).

[29] 'The talent myth: Are smart people overrated?' In: *the New Yorker* (22nd July 2002). URL: https://www.newyorker.com/magazine/2002/07/22/the-talent-myth.

[30] Alessandro Pluchino, Alessio Emanuele Biondo and Andrea Rapisarda. 'Talent versus luck: The role of randomness in success and failure'. In: *Advances in Complex systems* **21** (03n04) (2018): p. 1850014.

[31] Ben Cohen. *Winning a Nobel Prize Takes Luck as Much as Talent.* 6th Oct. 2022. URL: https://www.wsj.com/articles/nobel-prize-luck-success-talent-11664903787 (visited on 14/11/2022).

[32] J. Wiggins. *The Intelligent Fund Investor: Practical steps for better results in active and passive funds.* Harriman House Limited.

[33] Paul Ormerod. *Why Most Things Fail: Evolution, Extinction and Economics.* Pantheon, NY.

[34] Tomer Dean. 'The meeting that showed me the truth about VCs'. In: (2nd June 2017). URL: https://techcrunch.com/2017/06/01/the-meeting-that-showed-me-the-truth-about-vcs/ (visited on 12/05/2023).

[35] Gil Ben-Atzy. URL: https://www.slideshare.net/gilbenartzy/money-talks-things-you-learn-after-77-investment-rounds (visited on 20/04/2023).

[36] Jim Harter and Annamarie Mann. 'The right culture: Not just about employee satisfaction'. In: *Gallup Inc.* **20** (2017): p. 2019. URL: ht tps : / / www . gallup . com / workplace / 236366 / right - culture-not-employee-satisfaction.

[37] Robert Kegan and Lisa Lahey. *An Everyone Culture: Becoming a Deliberately Developmental Organisation.* Harvard Business Review Press.

[38] Jason Aten. URL: https://incafrica.com/library/jason- aten - this - was - steve - jobs - most - important - obser vation - when - he - returned - to - apple - it - changed - everything (visited on 14/11/2022).

[39] URL: https : / / www . unilever . com / news / news - search / 2020/putting-purpose-into-practice-our-covid-19- response/ (visited on 15/02/2023).

[40] D. Snowden et al. *Cynefin - Weaving Sense-Making Into the Fabric of Our World.* Cognitive Edge - The Cynefin Company.

[41] Ole Peters and Alexander Adamou. 'The ergodicity solution of the cooperation puzzle'. In: *Philosophical Transactions of the Royal Society A* **380** (2227) (2022): p. 20200425.

[42] O. Peters and M. Gell-Mann. 'Evaluating gambles using dynamics'. In: *Chaos: An Interdisciplinary Journal of Nonlinear Science* **26** (2) (Feb. 2016): p. 023103. ISSN: 1089-7682. DOI: 10 . 1063/1 . 4940236. URL: http://dx.doi.org/10.1063/1.4940236.

[43] Ole Peters and Alexander Adamou. *Ergodicity Economics Lecture Notes.* URL: ergodicityeconomics.com/lecture-notes/.

[44] Yonatan Berman, Ole Peters and Alexander Adamou. *Wealth Inequality and the Ergodic Hypothesis: Evidence from the United States.* 2020.

[45] Ole Peters and Alexander Adamou. *An evolutionary advantage of cooperation.* 2018. arXiv: 1506.03414.

[46] Steve Keen. *The New Economics.* Polity.

[47] David Sloan Wilson. *This view of life, Completing the Darwinian revolution.* Vintage.

[48] Adam Kahane. *Facilitating Breakthrough: How to Remove Obstacles, Bridge Differences, and Move Forward Together*. Berrett-Koehler Publishers.

[49] James Priest, Bernhard Bockelbrink and Liliana David. *Sociocracy 3.0*. URL: http://sociocracy30.org/ (visited on 22/12/2017).

[50] Noam Wasserman. *The Founder's Dilemmas*. Princeton University Press.

[51] B.H. Ong and M. Goyder. *Entrusted: Stewardship For Responsible Wealth Creation*. World Scientific Publishing Company.

[52] Graham Boyd et al. *Redesigning your economy with free companies that cannot be bought or sold, talk given in the Ellen MacArthur Foundation DIF programme*. 24th Nov. 2017. URL: https://www.thinkdif.co/sessions/redesigning-your-economy-free-companies-that-cannot-be-bought-or-sold.

[53] Simon Deakin. 'The Corporation as Commons: Rethinking Property Rights, Governance and Sustainability in the Business Enterprise'. In: *Queen's Law Journal* **37** (2) (2011): pp. 339–381.

[54] Rory Ridley-Duff. *The Case for FairShares: A New Model for Social Enterprise Development and the Strengthening of the Social and Solidarity Economy*. CreateSpace Independent Publishing Platform.

[55] Clayton Christensen, Jeffrey Dyer and Hal Gregersen. *The Innovator's DNA: Mastering the Five Skills of Disruptive Innovators*. Harvard Business Review Press.

[56] Bernhard Lietaer et al. *Money & Sustainability: the missing link (A report to the Club of Rome)*. Triarchy Press Ltd.

[57] Jim Brown. *Equity finance for social enterprises*. 2006.

[58] Jordan M. Barry, John William Hartfield and Scott Duke Kominers. 'On Derivatives Markets and Social Welfare: A Theory of Empty Voting and Hidden Ownership'. In: *Virginia Law Review* **99** (1103) (2013).

[59] Wolf-Georg Ringe. 'Empty Voting Revisited: The Telus Saga'. In: *University of Oxford Legal Research Paper Series* (Mar. 2013). SSRN-id2230528.

[60] Wolf-Georg Ringe. 'Hedge Funds and Risk-Decoupling — The Empty Voting Problem in the European Union'. In: *University of Oxford Legal Research Paper Series* (52) (Aug. 2012). SSRN-id2135489.

[61] Michael C. Schouten. 'The Mechanisms of Voting Efficiency'. In: *Columbia Business Law Review* 3 (2010).

[62] Alon Brav and Richmond D. Mathews. 'Empty Voting And The Efficiency Of Corporate Governance'. In: *AFA 2009 San Francisco Meetings Paper* (2010). SSRN-id1108632.

[63] David Yermack. 'Shareholder Voting and Corporate Governance'. In: *Annual Review of Financial Economics* 2 (1) (Mar. 2010): pp. 103–125.

[64] *The Modern Corporation: statement on company law*. URL: themoderncorporation.wordpress.com/company-law-memo/.

[65] Norman Wolfe. *The Living Organization: Transforming Business to Create Extraordinary Results*. Quantum Leaders Publishing.

[66] W.C. Kim and R. Mauborgne. *Blue Ocean Strategy, Expanded Edition: How to Create Uncontested Market Space and Make the Competition Irrelevant*. Harvard Business Review Press.

[67] Elinor Ostrom. *Governing the Commons: The Evolution of Institutions for Collective Action*. Cambridge University Press.

[68] John Fullerton. URL: https://capitalinstitute.org/finance-for-a-regenerative-world/ (visited on 20/04/2023).

[69] J. Montgomery and M. Van Clieaf. *Net Zero Business Models: Winning in the Global Net Zero Economy*. Wiley.

[70] Mariana Bozesan. 'Integral Investing: From Profit to Prosperity'. In: Springer International Publishing.

[71] Robert Dellner. *Integral Impact Investing*. Evolutesix Publishing.

[72] E. Poole. *Capitalism's Toxic Assumptions: Redefining Next Generation Economics*. Bloomsbury USA.

[73] R. Bookstaber. *The End of Theory: Financial Crises, the Failure of Economics, and the Sweep of Human Interaction*. Princeton University Press. ISBN: 9780691191850. URL: https://books.google.be/books?id=zViYDwAAQBAJ.

[74] Paul WB Atkins, David Sloan Wilson and Steven C Hayes. *Prosocial: Using evolutionary science to build productive, equitable, and collaborative groups*. New Harbinger Publications.

[75] Kate Raworth. *Doughnut Economics: Seven Ways to Think Like a 21st-Century Economist*. Chelsea Green Publishing.

[76] Frederik Laloux. *Reinventing organizations: A guide to creating organizations inspired by the next stage in human consciousness*. Nelson Parker, UK.

[77] URL: https://quoteinvestigator.com/2015/09/02/life-one/ (visited on 21/12/2022).

[78] Lawrence Ford. *The Secrets of the Seasons: You're Here for a Reason*. Conscious Capital Press. ISBN: 9781734844900.

[79] Alan Milburn. 12th Nov. 2022. URL: https://www.theguardian.com/commentisfree/2022/nov/12/7000-a-year-thats-hit-to-your-salary-if-you-come-from-a-working-class-family (visited on 14/11/2022).

[80] Steve Jobs. *Stanford commencement address*. 2005. URL: https://www.youtube.com/watch?v=UF8uR6Z6KLc (visited on 14/11/2022).

[81] J. Rawls. *A Theory of Justice*. Oxford Paperbacks 301 301. Harvard University Press.

[82] *Hopi Elders' Prophecy*. 8th June 2000. URL: https://www.awakin.org/v2/read/view.php?tid=702 (visited on 25/11/2022).

[83] Startup Genome. 'Global Startup Report 2019'. In: (). URL: https://startupgenome.com/reports/global-startup-ecosystem-report-2019 (visited on 16/05/2023).

[84] *Future Capital*. URL: https://www.futureofcapital.org/ (visited on 12/11/2022).

[85]   Maria-Vittoria Guarino et al. 'Sea-ice-free Arctic during the Last Interglacial supports fast future loss'. In: *Nature Climate Change* (Aug. 2020).

[86]   Judy Brown, Peter Soderbaum and Malgorzata Dereniowska. *Positional Analysis for Sustainable Development: Reconsidering policy, economics and accounting.* Vol. 46. Taylor & Francis.

[87]   *Ubuntu Philosophy.* URL: https://en.wikipedia.org/wiki/ Ubuntu_philosophy (visited on 25/11/2022).

Glossary

Actuality is what actually is. None of us can ever experience actuality directly and totally, rather each of us experiences our own unique reality.

Adaptive is used point at the need for deep growth or change. Perhaps to change who we are or our organisation's identity; or to grow our Size of Person by growing both our capacity for sense-making and our meaning-making stories. Often used as an adjective before the nouns Capacity, Way, Organisation, and Challenge.

Adaptive organisation refers to any organisation that is at least at Level 4 on all three axes, and striving towards Level 5 on each.

Antifragile lies beyond robustness and resilience. Antifragile is the capacity to grow stronger because of the stresses and headwinds you face.

Capital is something that has actual or perceived value. Examples include energy in nature, time and creativity in humans, relationships in society, manufactured capital, and of course financial capital. Every capital has an associated currency with it, e.g. money is the dominant currency of financial capital. In this book and *Rebuild* the six capitals of the Integrated Reporting Initiative are used:

- Natural (Terra);
- Human (Time, Energy, Quality Adjusted Life Year);
- Social and Relational (Reputation, connections);
- Intellectual (Number and ranking of citations, patents);
- Manufactured (Money, WIR, embodied energy);

- Financial (Money, WIR, local money-based currencies).

The examples of capital growth used in this book apply to any of these capitals. These examples use a stripped-down, minimalist definition of capital as a narrow lens, highlighting what matters to understand the central point: capital grows non-ergodically. This remains true in the specific definitions of most of the capitals in the finance sector, in biology, or in the social sciences.

Cargo Cult / Scientism we use narrowly for the superficial application of science, or dressing opinions up in the language of science, without scientific rigour. This is at best naively harmful, at worst malicious manipulation. Scientism in our usage is synonymous with cargo cults. Richard Feynman named these rituals cargo cults after the Melanesian Islanders. As WW2 raged, they first saw Japanese planes bringing supplies, then American planes. Not understanding what was actually happening (a world war, the nature of flight, etc.) they began following rituals patterned on what they saw the troops doing before a plane brought supplies. Of course, flattening a length of ground, building a hut in the middle, and wearing coconut shells fashioned to look like headphones is not going to cause an aeroplane with supplies to materialise! As of December 2022[2], 500 people in the village of Lamakara on the island of Tanna are still adherents of one of these cargo cults.

Complementary pairs also called conjugate pairs are central to quantum physics. These are two apparently different entities that have a deeper relationship. They may even be perceived as mutually exclusive. Position and momentum, particles and waves are common in physics. Actuality is filled with complementary pairs.

Currency is a tool used to attribute, store, or trade in the value of an associated capital. Each capital has one or more intrinsic currencies that fully reflects the nature and value of that capital. So time is best reflected in a time currency, not in money; energy in an energy currency, not in money; and only positive interest debt is correctly represented with money. Money is often confused with currency; and in some

[2]https://en.wikipedia.org/wiki/John_Frum

Here

usages our definitions of money and currency are swapped.

Economy (An) is a tool used to do the job of provisioning; i.e., transporting a capital from where it is abundant to where it is needed.

Ecosystem, a strongly connected is a set of entities, eg. businesses, where the businesses in the ecosystem share common pools of capitals, have interlocking governance structures and interactions, and are sufficiently diverse. An ecosystem can be deemed strongly connected if the companies in it, and the ecosystem as a whole, have sufficient strength in both the systems and the interactivity to begin approaching the ergodic limit.

Emergent strategy (or anything emergent) is one that cannot be defined completely and precisely and then followed as is. You can think of an emergent strategy as a second-order, or even higher-order strategy loop, where the optimum operating strategy only can be formulated right at the moment you need to use it. You can find more in our book *Rebuild*.

Ergodic Investment Strategy is an ergodic strategy specifically designed to optimise the outcomes of investments of capital. Clearly for financial capital, but equally relevant for investments of any of the six capitals.

Ergodic Limit is the maximum possible growth rate in a capital. It is only achievable when the dynamics of the processes growing or shrinking the capital are completely ergodic. For geometric, or multiplicative capital growth dynamics, this is only reached with either zero variance in the process (everything is completely predictable) or 100% pooling and redistribution of the capitals across a sufficiently large, sufficiently diverse, strongly connected ecosystem of companies.

Ergodic Strategy is one taking into account the non-ergodic nature of most business and economic processes. Each business, business unit, and product is one connected path, and has the sensitivity to unpredictables that that non-ergodic nature causes. An ergodic strategy will have a competitive edge over a traditional strategy because it correctly predicts the risks and returns caused by the losses multiplicative dynamics actually have, versus the simplistic approach to business planning currently used. The more the ergodic strategy makes optimum use of the ecosystemic levers to reduce this risk by shifting the dynamics closer to full ergodicity, the bigger the competitive edge over today's traditional strategies.

Ergodicity is what you have if random events happening in a sequence have the same expected value as the same random events happening independently. Technically, the ensemble average is the same as the time / path average. Ergodicity is not true for most business activities, and our lives: the time average is very different to the ensemble average we were taught to use.

FairShares Commons is a set of functionalities and patterns yielding one way of constructing a free company well suited to building a regenerative, net positive, circular etc. Economy of the Free. A FairShares Commons can be built in many ways using existing types of companies in jurisdictions around the world; it is not one legal form. A FairShares Commons includes all relevant stakeholders in governance and wealth sharing, and is inherently a protected commons for the benefit of current and future generations of stakeholders. Stakeholders can include abstract institutions like cities, nations, the environment, etc.

Job 1 is what someone is hired to do, their job description, and the more of their human capital they invest in this (intellectual, time, effort, relationships) the better the beneficial return for the business on their human capital investment, and hence on the financial capital invested as an enabler. Job 2 Is everything else that a person does in the company to protect themselves from their colleagues, to look good in front of their subordinates, peers, and managers, and to continue to be accepted as a member of the tribe.

Lens refers to everything and anything you use in constructing your experienced reality out of actuality. The lens(es) you use pre-determine the reality you can construct by hiding some parts of actuality, magnifying others, and distorting all. Choose your lenses wisely (though you may not be free to choose in the context you are in) to bring what is important into sharp focus, and hide what is unimportant noise. Never imagine that you experience what actually is—your lenses are always present.

Meaning-making is the final step, after sense-making, in constructing your internally experienced reality. You use your meaning-making templates, or stories, to give meaning to what you have taken in of actuality.

Rational from the Latin word for reason, it means the capacity to logically think through a situation to connect facts with premises. So an economic agent is rational if their behaviour is congruent with their overall objectives. Neoclassical economics constricts rationality to maximising self-interest.

Reality is, in our narrow usage here, your inner experienced reality. Your reality comes from the limited elements of actuality absorbed, filtered, and modified by your senses. It is then shaped or distorted by your nature, sense-making, and meaning-making. So each of us experiences a unique reality. None of us can ever directly experience all actuality, nor another's reality.

Regenerative and Net Positive business grows all the capitals it touches, in particular natural and human capitals. A regenerative business is designed to intrinsically multiply all capitals it touches, in an antifragile way.

Sense-making is the second step in constructing your experienced reality. Sense-making is using your capacity for logical and post-logical thought forms to assemble the puzzle-pieces you have taken in, prior to your attributing meaning using your meaning-making stories. The smaller your capacity, the less actuality you take in, and the more you distort it to fit into your capacity. The limits to your capacity for sense-making limit the meaning you can make, and hence the reality you experience.

Theory A theory, in strict usage in science, unlike in daily language, is the current best falsifiable description of what we can say about how the world works; one that has survived multiple attempts using rigorous processes to prove false. Conventional daily usage is synonymous with an hypothesis or phenomenological model in science.

Thought forms, dialectic / post logical / post rational are the 28 different thought forms that we begin developing after we have mastered sufficient logical thinking. These forms of thought are based on opposites, and are vital to grasp aspects of actuality that run counter to binary logic.

Ubuntu Ubuntu is a word and concept in the Nguni Bantu language family. It's variously translated as 'I am because we are', 'I am because you are', or 'humanity towards others' (in Zulu 'umuntu ngumuntu ngabantu'), and in the philosophical sense is 'the belief in a universal bond of sharing that connects all humanity'[87].

Index

INDEX

six, 117
cargo cult, xii, 92, 106
cause-effect, xiii, 34
CCA Partners, xii
Chaebol, 49
charity, 21
China, 50
CHW or WIR currency, 122
civilisation, collapse, 121
climate change, 58, 102, 113
cognitive dissonance, 108
collaborating, 121
Collaborating with the Enemy, 114
Collaboratingwith the Enemy, 94
collaboration, viii, ix, xv, 4, 24, 48, 50, 53, 55, 57, 69, 73, 89, 91, 93, 94, 101, 114, 124
collaboration and competition, 24, 50, 81, 93, 101
nature, 94
collaboration-competition space, 55, 56
Commons, x
of productive capacity, 82, 123
company
strong, 54
weak, 53
competition, 24, 50, 93
complementary pair, 21, 43, 46, 58, 74, 129
compromise, x, 87, 102
forced, 45, 55, 79
Conscious Capitalism, x
consent, 78
cooperative, xii, 49, 84
multi-stakeholder, 84

countercyclical, 55, 78, 98
Covid-19, 2–3, 47, 48
Curie, Marie, 11, 126
currency, 86
complementary, 83, 86
Cynefin, 55

DAO, x, xiv, 78, 81
FairShares Commons, 81
Daoism, 4
Darwin, 60, 92–93
default mode network, 108
democracy, deep, 81
Diamond, Jared, xv
diversity, 54, 95, 98, 113
requisite, 122
dots, connect the, 110
driver statement, 83

economics, xi, xii, 5, 19, 24, 59, 62, 63, 101, 102, 104
doughnut, 87, 102, 118
regenerative, 118
rethinking, 102
economy
blue, x
circular, x, 87, 95, 102
regenerative, x, 87, 95, 100, 102
ecosystems
company, 89, 125
ecosystem of, 56
natural, 90, 95
six strata of, 76, 77
strongly connected, 57, 96
eggs and bacon, 20, 21
Elkington, John, x

155